There was once a city perched on a rock. There was and there still is. It has taken me sixty years to discover the soul of the city, and then I am only at the beginning. Every street, every building, has a story to tell. The city is a house of many rooms.

What we find speaks to us, past and present.

ORVIETO AS IT WAS... AND IS

A Personal Journal

To those whose heart has already been captured by this city on a rock and to those for whom this is a "first time"

by Erika Pauli Bizzarri

ORVIETO AS IT WAS... AND IS

A Personal Journal

Copyright © 2020 by Erika Pauli Bizzarri

ISBN - 978-1-716-35565-3

All rights reserved.

No part of this book may be reproduced in any form by any electronic or mechanical means including photocopying, recording, or information storage and retrieval without permission in writing from the author.

Printed in U.S.A

CONTENTS:

Introduction 8
Ancient history and the first Etruscan city................................. 11
Subterranean Orvieto and its caves... 24
Coat of arms - the city's visiting card – Calvino, Invisible Cities......... 29
Morning cappuccino, people and dogs....................................... 30
The people who are – and were 35
Italian holidays – the Miracle of 1264 36
Orvieto, free Commune, Monaldeschi and Filippeschi 41
Church of Sant'Andrea, papal politics, Pranzo di Ferragosto 43
Epiphany, manger scenes, Befana, an Italian Christmas.......... 46
Palomba, City Hall 49
Via Garibaldi, partisans and painters, master masons and nuns........ 50
San Lorenzo, catering school, words... 52
Library and Marino Moretti, back to Piazza Ranieri 54
Piazza della Repubblica, City Hall, Ippolito Scalza 56
Bar Montanucci and the Italian espresso; Gualverio Michelangeli...... 57
Erika's shop: crafts and artisans 60
Piazza della Legna, dell'Erba, Loggia dei Mercanti, the Templars 62
Palazzo del Gusto/Vino, wine tasting, American Thanksgiving......... 64
Via Malabranca, Catherine de' Medici....................................... 67
Sant'Agostino and Mochi, Ippolito Scalza, San Giovenale 72
Via della Cava, the Well, the festivals 75
Pope Boniface VIII 79
Funicular, Cozza, Garibaldi, Jews and Muslims, St.Patrick's Well 80
Via Roma and military barracks, San Domenico...................... 84
American Study abroad programs, Via Pecorelli....................... 89
Cavour, Palazzo dei Sette, Palazzo del Popolo 91
Mancinelli Theater, the Corso, Servite church 95
Via del Duomo, heart of Orvieto, Palazzo Netti, San Giuseppe 98
Clock Tower, plague, cathedral workyard, Marino Moretti 102
The Duomo, Maitani, Cathars 107

The Cathedral and its frescoes, names, the Miracle of Bolsena 114
Ippolito Scalza, Gentile da Fabriano and pastries 120
World War II and the saving of Orvieto 125
Signorelli and the End of the World 127
Cathedral Museum and Henry VIII 133
What Orvieto is for me 140
Those who are no longer here 144
Orvieto. City of high bastions 146
Ring around the cliff, the Badia, the cemetery, the surroundings 147
What Orvieto means to one student 154
Suggested reading 156
Acknowledgments 158

Disclaimer

This book is both a guide book and a memoir. It reflects the author's (my) present recollections of experiences over time. Memory may have its own story to tell but I relate the facts as I best remember them. Some of the information comes from personal sources and actual conversations, and some from previously printed material. The dialogue recreated is completely imaginary.

My heartfelt thanks to all the wonderful friends I have made here throughout the years and if these personal reflections have in any way upset them or their families, it has been unintentional and I realize that their memories may be different from my own.

"Help, I got lost in Orvieto!
Impossible you might say, improbable I answer...
True, the city seems to be too small to lose your way in, if by that you mean following your feet to get from one place to another. But when you have the courage to wander aimlessly, to do something different... in other words get lost ... you'll find yourself in an unknown lane, passing an anonymous doorway with its paint peeling off, leading to a sunless courtyard... illuminated suddenly by a ray of light... Getting lost is what you're after... just every so often, no risk involved, for you know you'll always find your way back."

James Lalonde

Orvieto rising out of the fog - Picture by Erika Bizzarri

INTRODUCTION
Italian identity, what was and is

This city on the rock, immortalized in countless photos, is so much more than just a view from afar. "Orvieto" is what it's called on the map, "Urbsvetus" is what it was called a thousand years ago, "Velzna" is what it was called two thousand years ago. So perhaps before you discover the city for yourself, a word or two about myself and why I hope you will also fall in love with what has been home to me for almost sixty years. A lifetime, you might say.

It is sort of like the two sides of a coin, obverse and reverse. From where I live I see it from a distance, an island rising from the fog. But then when I go down into the valley and up to the city itself, my point of view changes as I look back over the valley to where I live as I join the host of others who once walked these streets – Etruscans, cardinals and popes – as well as the common people who now walk them every day and wouldn't want to live elsewhere.

As we exchange greetings, it is they who make me realize I am not invisible. It might be my lawyer friend, who is always reading some ancient Roman author and can't wait to tell me about it. Or Don Marcello, whose bride is the church of Sant'Andrea. Or the teller from the bank.

You may wonder though how I ended up here, why an American who grew up on a farm in Massachusetts and studied and lived in New York now calls Orvieto home. To begin with, there's the fact that my Italian husband was an archaeologist and was appointed archaeological director of the Orvieto office. Then my older son has followed in his father's footsteps and is also an archaeologist. And my younger son has never wanted to go anywhere else.

Indeed both are truly part of this town. When I was in the hospital just after giving birth to Lamberto, my second son, Claudio, who was five at the time, was walking with his father and said: "you know Mamma is American, Lamberto is Orvietano, you and I are Perugini," (for both he and his father were born in Perugia and that is what counts in Italy), establishing a bond of just the two of them.

Orvieto, the city on a rock. Whether you are coming by train or car or even on foot, it is more than just another hilltop town, perched up on high. It's a life style, a refuge for expats, a place that slowly steals into your heart, and if you were born and grew up here, it's a place you want to keep calling home.

Everyone you ask has their own definition of Orvieto:

For Mastro Mechoro, a thirteenth-century poet –
a rock reaching up to the clouds in the sky

For Fazio degli Uberti, a fourteenth-century poet –
a city high and strange

For Carmel, an Australian soprano – *a magnet*

For Wladimiro Giulietti, former mayor of Orvieto –
his "grande amore"

For Valeriano Venturi, a lawyer –
fragrance of linden trees and smell of rain on hot cobblestones

For Jean Chelnov, a journalist –
a jewel to be saved

For Reno Montanucci -
the city - teller of tales, the many-layered city

For Mario Piccione, Geosonda engineer –
the Rock is queen. We are the servants

For the Orvietani in general –
the Rock, the city of Corpus Domini.
A hunk of tufa surrounded by lots of air

And when all is said and done, above all there's the human factor. As we wander the streets we can conjure up the ghosts of centuries past: Larth the Etruscan, Arnolfo di Cambio, Lorenzo Maitani, Luca Signorelli, Ippolito Scalza, and various and sundry popes, those who made Orvieto what it was and is. We can reach out to those who, year after year, return to renew friendships and remind them there is still so much they have previously been unaware of. It is to them, as well as the first-time visitor, that this is dedicated.

There are countless aspects to be discovered by the discerning visitor. You can concentrate on a particular period or style, or see just who the visitors are and why they come. But to understand the "now" of a city we have to go to its past, to where it came from. And as human beings, one of our distinguishing characteristics is curiosity.

THE BEGINNINGS
Ancient history and the first Etruscan city: Larth, the Etruscan; archaeological museums and digs

One of the first questions that comes to mind – depending perhaps on whether you're arriving from the south or from the north – is just what made this site, a sort of island in the sea of a plain between the Apennines on one side and the uplands towards Lazio on the other, so alluring. Now if you were to found a city, what would your prerequisites be? Certainly, it would have had to be easy to defend, far from the nefarious vapors and mists of the lowlands, and with a good source of water. But the first inhabitants of around 2500 years ago were not discouraged by the lack of water up on this plateau and found ways to solve the problem. Orvieto Underground will show you how they did it.

So perhaps reference to the city's Etruscan past is in order. Arriving by car and following indications for the railroad station before starting your climb up to the city, you may have passed the sign that says Necropolis of Crocifisso del Tufo, halfway up to the top of the plateau. It's as good a way as any to enter the city's past.

As my husband, whose ancestors on his father's side came from Orvieto, wrote in his book *Magica Etruria:* "This city resembles no other, and the same holds for its necropolis. Best though to avoid the noisy crowd, or the mediocre advantage of a guided tour. Best to be by yourself if you wish to dialogue with your surroundings."

You may feel he is right, but as my granddaughter also pointed out, sharing is important, for then you see things you might not have noticed otherwise. In the necropolis, the Etruscan past is more than immanent. It is real and alive – and that holds for the various pasts of this city of Orvieto. The ghosts of former centuries are simply waiting for you to lay aside the preoccupations that accompany your daily life so they may come and keep you company. Once the transitory visitors have left, and the Orvietani themselves have withdrawn into the fantasy world of television, the time has come to take up the underlying thread of that frenetic adventure of the unchangeable, eternally renewable human adventure that is Orvieto.

Orvieto, or *Velzna* (its Etruscan name), is one of the most loquacious of Etruscan cities. But who, you may ask, were the Etruscans? In pre-Roman times the Italic peninsula, not yet Italy, was home to countless tribes – Latins, Sabines, Umbrians, the Plestini, to mention just a few. Then there were the Greeks who colonized the southern part of the peninsula and Sicily. In central Italy we have the Etruscans, some of whom lived in what we now call Orvieto, the emblematic city of the Etruscan league, from around the ninth century BC till 264 BC when they were defeated by the Romans. There has long been a debate as to whether the famed *Fanum Voltumnae*, the federal Etruscan sanctuary where the member cities met, was located here, but the discovery of temples and processional roads in the plain below the cliff seems to have convinced even those who once thought otherwise.

Today it is the cemeteries and tombs of the Etruscans that tell us what their life was like. There is indeed something unique about the necropolis of Crocifisso del Tufo, this city of the dead, with small mostly one-room "apartments" lining streets set out in a grid plan, mirroring that of the city up above and its relatively egalitarian composition. What we are wandering through is only a part of the ring of tombs that circled the base of the cliff. As we go from one street to another, run your hands over the inscriptions above each doorway, most of them read from right to left. They give us the name of the owner, the equivalent of "James Jones" or "Marilyn Brown". My husband Mario was very attuned to this world of the past.

"One almost expects the rhythmic activities of daily life to start up from one moment to the next, with people bustling in the streets, the regular beat of the metal worker's hammer, the gay voices of children calling from door to door. We can feel the presence of the men who labored and sweated to build these "houses", reflecting the layout of the living city above." Velzna seems to have been peopled by a practical merchant

caste, by people who knew how to read and write and were proud of the fact, and not the conservative aristocracies of southern Etruria whose tombs contained fabulous jewelry. These inscriptions reveal that the family names were not all Etruscan. In other words a Latin, an Oscan, an Umbrian and even a Celt could adopt Velzna as his home and become a citizen and even a member of the upper classes. Evidently not all that much has changed, when we think of the "foreigners" -- Moldavians and Hungarians, Albanians, Scottish, Australians, English and Americans, Germans and Dutch -- who have come and settled here recently and have become citizens of this Italian hill town of Orvieto.

Oh, look, there's Larth, the Etruscan, waiting for us halfway up one of the streets. True he's not very tall and you might think his nose is a bit large, his physique is clearly that of a man used to wielding arms. He's not alone, of course, but he's the spokesman for the group.

"Come," he says. "Let me show you something. While I fought bravely for my people, what was meant to remember me, to pay me honor, is no longer here. It sits by itself in a space of its own in what they call a museum. But that is because it was moveable. If we address my companions here, they will tell you that this tomb or that was where their bodies were laid. Almost all are still remembered by their names. Mi - I am the tomb of . . . most often we can read them going from right to left. Mi aveles sipanas. Or it might be the name of a woman. Yet that was not the fate of all. See that brief inscription above this entrance to a tomb? It is now just a single word: AISIAS. Yet if you run your hand along the word you can feel a gouged out area where a longer inscription has been chiseled away. The tomb is now dedicated to the gods, AISIAS. This was where my friend, a haruspex, a priest, who interpreted their will, found his last resting place. He had displeased them and his name was removed from human memory. The pitcher with a hole in the bottom so that the sacrificial wine could sink into the earth was part of his paraphernalia."

"Of course each tomb has its story. That small box-like structure over there, for instance, is where my little four-year old cousin was buried – her life was all too short. A whole set of miniature vases were made

specifically to accompany her to the underworld. But our fates were set before we were born."

"Or look up at some of these rooms where the roof is still more or less intact. Can't you see the workers laying row of projecting row of blocks till all that was needed to finish it off was one keystone at the top? There are even handholds in that final block."

Larth the Etruscan - Courtesy of Fondazione per il Museo "Claudio Faina"

The Etruscans had a deep-rooted respect for burials in this city of the dead. When they encountered a previous grave as they were building a new "apartment," they would piously collect the bones and offerings and provide them with new housing in miniature.

Larth once more wants to tell us something:

"I was watching when your workers began removing the earth that had covered this city of the dead for so many centuries. And I appreciate the fact that you too respected the dead, salvaging every small fragment of pottery. I was particularly fond of that tall man with a beard, so much

taller than most of us Etruscans, whose name was Checco. He was delighted when he found something that had not been smashed by the disrespectful Romans.
Then there was that shorter man, who seemed to be more than just a workman, since he gave orders. He would have seemed a typical one of us, reclining on the cover of a sarcophagus, showing off his generous stomach. They called him Beppe. There was also that strange woman with voluminous white skirts and a dark headdress, who, I am told, was devoted to her god. Climbing up and down ladders was not simple for her. Of course there was also the man everyone deferred to who was in charge of it all. They addressed him as dottore. How excited he was when he found that black bucchero pitcher in the shape of a human-headed bird. And then there was that little fellow, I could tell he felt he was one of us."

The Romans however, particularly the soldiers besieging the city for well over two years, paid scant attention to such niceties. Plundering the tombs may have been just one of their perks, where, if they were lucky, they might find objects in gold, meant to accompany the deceased to the underworld. Tomb robbers have always thrived in places like the Orvieto countryside. Divining rods were still used to identify empty spaces as late as the mid-twentieth century. A necropolis like Orvieto was of course a prime target. In the nineteenth century, tunnels were dug underground along the facades of the tombs, at the time covered with earth and detritus thrown down from the top of the cliff. When an empty space was encountered, where the vault had not collapsed, the tomb could be entered, and objects in gold or painted imported vases purloined for the antique market. It was a dangerous undertaking to which the finding of the skeleton of a boy of about fourteen bears witness. Being small, he had been sent ahead to see which tomb was still empty and the tunnel he was in collapsed. Yet there were also burials under the streets themselves. One that tomb robbers had missed contained a skeleton, identified as that of a woman by her kitchen knife. She was still there intact, lying on her funeral bed, when my husband opened the tomb, but her bones soon turned to dust. That year the American crew of student diggers had had a car with a Virginia license plate. The workers had been convinced it was a sign that we would find a "virgin" tomb, and we did!

There's a small room near the ticket office, dedicated to Mario Bizzarri, my husband, with explanatory panels (in English) to be read before visiting the tombs. Other panels by the tombs themselves give you an insight into what the site once looked like and what was found there. If you're here in summer when a dig is going on, funded by the non-profit Sostratos, you can even hold a piece of 2,500-year-old pottery and run your fingers over the surface, or watch as the fragments are being cleaned, catalogued and assembled. You can also pick up a few apples or plums that litter the ground in season, and which no one knows what to do with. Well, no one except me, and I have made several apple pies for volunteers and students intent on washing the potsherds, or pottery fragments, unearthed in the dig.

If your curiosity has been aroused and you decide to continue on the tracks of the Etruscans, the next step might be the ruins of the Etruscan temple of Belvedere next to the funicular station that brings visitors and schoolchildren to the top of the plateau. You can park you car there, too, in Piazza Cahen and then use your imagination to transform these blocks of stone into a temple with a colonnaded portico, an entrance only on the front and three chambers for the divinities in the back. We are, however, humans, and what distinguishes us is our capacity for imagination.

Further information on the past comes from the archaeological museums, and "Orvieto Underground", where the distant past merges with the more recent past. So once you have taken note of the temple, you can either step up on the minibus to Piazza Duomo, or take a ten-minute walk to the center of town and the Cathedral, past the school where children in their smocks are waiting for their parents to pick them up. I rather like the idea of smocks for it creates a certain social equality among the children. Black for boys and white for girls, with a big blue or pink bow at the collar.

There are two archaeological museums – the Claudio Faina Museum across from the cathedral, and the National Archaeological Museum in one of the papal palaces to the right of the cathedral.

Both of these museums deal primarily with the Etruscans, who dominated this part of the Italic peninsula until they were vanquished by the Romans. Indeed, the Etruscan Tarquins were the last kings of Rome. Much of what we find in Roman culture harks back to Etruscan forebears, such as the *fasces* or bundle of rods with an axe in the middle, the origin of the term fascism. The symbol even appears in various US contexts, including the Mercury dime.

If you're not a specialist, examining the objects in a museum may give you only a superficial picture of what mattered to the Etruscans, and how they lived. But look at it this way: a collection is also of interest in what it reveals or conceals of the secret motivation that led to its creation, saving these objects from dispersion, from being lost in the slipstream of time. As Italo Calvino notes in his book of essays

Collection of Sand, "Just like every collection, this one is a diary as well: a diary of travels, of course, but also of feelings, states of mind, moods... The fascination of a collection lies just as much in what it reveals as in what it conceals of the secret urge that led to its creation." — from Italo Calvino, *Collection of Sand, 1984.*

As you go up the steps to the Claudio Faina Museum, you are probably asking yourself who in the world this Claudio Faina was, and why he was so interested in collecting. The palazzo itself is an example of a private home of a patrician family, begun in 1846 on the site of a thirteenth-century house that had belonged to the Monaldeschi, one of the leading families in the city at the time. Now, however, look for Claudio Faina in his study, where he and Count Mauro and his nephew Eugenio may still be excitedly discussing a new coin just discovered on the market. Or they may be marveling over an Attic vase, a black-figure amphora or water jar, imported from Athens -- a sign of prestige for its owner. Or a breathtakingly thin black *bucchero kylix* or drinking cup, that had seen the light after more than two thousand years when workers carefully brushed away the earth in the new digs in the necropolis at the base of the cliff.

Speaking of bucchero, that specifically Etruscan type of pottery the finest pieces were shiny black, with a metallic sheen. But the pieces in the tombs were mostly thicker and gray in color, not as well fired, let's say an inferior quality that was used as a funerary offering. When my husband was teaching a course on the Etruscans to American students in Florence, he invited one young woman to come down for the summer and help out at the Faina museum. Her task one day was to wash some bucchero shards. Carolyn Valone, who later became a well-known art historian, put some in the sink to soak so it would be easier to get the dirt off. Half an hour later she went to wash them and felt around in the water. My God, where had they gone? There was nothing but sludge. They had dissolved! She was frantic since Mario was off somewhere doing something else. When she tracked him down and confessed, he just laughed and said they had too many grey bucchero shards around anyway.

Erika at dig - Photo by Mario Bizzarri

Mario was already working to organize the Faina museum when our son was born. Word got around that we had named him Claudio for Claudio Faina. That hadn't even occurred to us for we had just looked for a name that would sound good in English as well as Italian. Besides which we had thought it would be a girl, whom we would have called Claudia.

The nineteenth century saw interest in the Etruscans come to the fore, with guidebooks such as Mrs. Hamilton Gray's *Tour to the Sepulchres of Etruria* in 1839 and the incomparable *Cities and Cemeteries of Etru-*

ria by George Dennis. Perhaps interest in the Etruscans was sparked in particular by D.H. Lawrence and his *Etruscan Places*. I think, however, there must also be something in my family's DNA, for besides now having a son who is an archaeologist and whose father is still cited for his ground-breaking studies on Orvieto, with, in turn, his grandfather who was an inspector of antiquities, my own great-grandfather on my father's side, a Pauli, had also drawn up an encyclopedia of Etruscan inscriptions. When I was attending Columbia University, I thought I would look up his work in the New York City Library, and sure enough it was there.

Claudio Faina will undoubtedly invite you to go to the upper floor and marvel at the vases painted with black or red figures. The shapes of Greek pottery tell you what they were used for. An amphora was used for carrying water or holding wine at the banquets, the *kylix* was for drinking, the *hydria* for drawing water. The visitor may be surprised to learn that more Attic vases, made to order for the Etruscans, have been found in Etruria than in Greece. The Etruscans, however, also made their own versions of the Greek black-figure and red-figure pottery. If your knowledge of Greek mythology needs to be refreshed, don't worry, for the panels and captions are all in English.

Subjects often deal with the exploits of the heroes and gods, warriors leaving for battle on their chariots, with Athena and the other gods accompanying them, and events from the Trojan War, reflecting what the Etruscans found of interest. Some subjects though, are more mundane. When the museum was solemnly inaugurated in 1958 by a cardinal, my husband rushed to move one of the chalice cups with an explicitly erotic scene to a lower shelf, behind "closed doors."

The warrior's head on the ground floor, across from the ticket office, is the funeral monument of Larth, the Etruscan, with whose spirit we have already conversed. The name is uncommon and possibly indicates that Larth was a foreign mercenary who settled in *Velzna*. Encased in his helmet, he silently observes the sarcophagus across the way where a fellow Etruscan reclines, holding his patera or offering dish. Scenes taken from the Iliad and the Odyssey are on the other large sarcophagus and still have traces of color. That grimacing face with fangs in the showcase in the next room is a gorgon, somehow fearfully beautiful, who kept watch over the entrance to the temple. And that small standing female figure in a case all her own may not meet your standards of beauty even if she is called a Venus.

Scholars have long been debating as to whether she might originally have been a he, a kouros, or nude male youth. The marble is undoubtedly Greek, yet in the fifth century BC the Greeks were still more interested in portraying the male nude. She was found in Cannicella, on the south side of Orvieto, both a necropolis and sanctuary connected to water (since water comes from underground it often refers to the underworld). On high are temple decorations, with the series of antefixes, shell-shaped coverings for the ends of the beams, which were cast from a matrix. The nude body of the central figure from the pediment or gable, on the right-hand wall, is particularly sensuous. Then don't miss the marvelous small terracotta head of a man fingering his beard. Until recently you might have run across the twentieth-century "twin" of this man who lived 2500 years ago sitting on a bench in one of the piazzas, fingering his cane. Now however he and his twin are probably comparing notes on how *Velzna*/Orvieto has changed.

Even though they're not Etruscan, while they and you are here in the museum, you might as well take note of the two medieval statues of Pope Boniface VIII. There'll be more about him later.

Be sure to go up to the other floors to see the Etruscan bronzes and ceramic production. And do wander along the upper corridor where windows frame the stunning Orvieto cathedral across the way. You can feel you're a sort of Brobdingnagian Gulliver looking down at the Lilliputian humans in the square in front of the great frontispiece of the church, with its mosaic stories.

The National Archaeological Museum in one of the papal palaces to the right of the cathedral can give you a more comprehensive picture of the Etruscan civilization. Although there are few explanations in English, just keep in mind what you've learned from the Faina Museum. Even if you don't manage to get to the hills just outside Orvieto, the frescoes from two of the painted tombs in Porano, transferred to this museum, can give you an idea of the daily life of the Etruscans. They depict the banquet with men and women reclining on their couches and servants kneading bread and preparing the roast for the banquet. The fact that the names of the servants are written next to them, indicates that these "slaves" were not just chattel, but were considered people, with names of their own. One feels like saying: *"move over on that couch, make room for me."* The ritual of a shared meal -- how important that still is: the roast pig or porchetta as a sort of symbol for Orvieto, the chestnuts and new wine in autumn, the grilled sausages in winter!

Do also glance at the artifacts uncovered in the latest excavations at the Necropoli, and at the so-called Campo della Fiera, with its temples and tombs. This was *Fanum Voltumnae*, where the meetings of the twelve most important cities of the Etruscan league were held until the Romans starved the city of *Velzna* on the cliff into surrender in 264 BC. The base of a statue, no longer there, dating to the sixth century BC seems to call up its donor. Perhaps she was waiting for us, for there she is proudly hovering over the large stone base.

"Oh yes, I was a slave but became a freedwoman and took the name of the clan of my former owner, Larecenas. Arunth Pinies, who was a member of the elite, married me, and I knew how to read and write and had property of my own, as other Etruscan women did. In gratitude I, Kanuta, offered a statue to Tluschva, and commemorated it with an inscription, although, alas, the Romans plundered it along with 2000 other bronzes when they defeated my city. Touch this stone and make an offering to Tluschva when you go by."

Even after the Etruscans had been driven out, the Romans continued to venerate gods at the site. That hoard of coins in the showcase was found in the stone container on the floor below, where they had been inserted through the slit in the stone lid. Coins can be dated, depending in particular on whatever emperor they picture. So we know just who frequented this site.

If you can get there (again if the dig is in progress), you will find, spread out over an area that gets larger every year, the foundations of temples along a processional route, the later additions of Roman baths, and tombs of all sorts. They present us with a kaleidoscope of the life and death of the inhabitants of the city, up through medieval times. Of particular note are the foundations of a Franciscan church of which the whereabouts had been lost. Portions of an early Christian mosaic floor, and later tombs probably dating to the time of the Black Death, when the church was abandoned, bring it back to life. To peel away the layers of history is always fascinating, and that can still be done, even if the dig itself is closed. I was in the museum one afternoon when an American couple wandered in, so I offered to tell them what they were looking at. If I hadn't, how little it would all have meant to them.

What a dig is like comes through in the following description of a day at the necropolis of Cannicella on the southern side of the cliff with unexpected finds that give you a glimpse of the past. I described it in a letter to a friend of mine, Jean Chelnov, a journalist who was writing an article called *The Saving of a Jewel* for the magazine GEO, after landslides had threatened the city on top of the cliff, and the Italian government had allocated a substantial sum for the cities of Orvieto and Todi to shore up the crumbling cliffs. This was when money was still available for projects of this sort, for nowadays the outer layers of tufa that porous yellowish rock of volcanic origins, would still be peeling off like an onionskin, gradually eroded by wind and water.

"Report from Orvieto. Grand Tour travelers described it as a strange city, that looked threatening and menacing when they came close to its looming cliff, especially in the almost dusk, when the houses rise up a livid color against a smoke dark sky and the lights of the houses and streets make it seem a castle to be taken, a sorcerer's castle. Or when you see it from Cannicella, where the canes surround the base and then the cliff rises up straight and seems to deny approach to the city on the top, which from here cannot even be seen. All descriptions that hold for the city today as they did a couple of hundred years ago. Cannicella continues to have many a tale to tell. An Etruscan sanctuary and cemetery – that we knew. In a cistern Claudio (my archaeologist son) had come across a Roman or early post-Roman tomb of a child, finding fragments of the tiny fragile skeleton and the coin that was put in its mouth to

ensure its trip to the other world. But other things as well it has to tell. I told you that Claudio (and their colleagues Alba and Pier Luigi) have been excavating the spots where the supports for the new shed roof are to go. And in one of them they came across a tomb. A poor tomb. A simple rectangular shape consisting of rough-cut uneven stones. Something bronze seemed to emerge. Then slowly the skull and the jawbone with its teeth – good teeth he had. For it was a man. The bronze seems to have been part of a belt – and on one side the remains of an iron spear or dagger. From the type of belt buckle and the decorations, the absence of pottery and the simplicity of the burial, it is probably Late Antique, perhaps the tomb of a Goth. Perhaps one of those Belisarius besieged in "Ourbeventus" and finally drove out. His leg bones have been uncovered – the Goth's I mean – and they are very straight. My mother says he probably didn't spend much time on horseback then. So far no arms, no rib cage. Tomorrow they will continue excavating. Today they carefully uncovered the belt buckle, made a cast of some things, took parts out of the tomb, safely supported by plaster. Tomorrow we will see what else comes out. The fact that it is not an Etruscan tomb but later makes it all the more interesting. For it means that the site continued to be hallowed – continued to be used as a burial site."

It turned out to be a Lombard tomb of the sixth century and the dagger was of the type known as *scramasax*, used by the Frankish and Germanic peoples.

Subterranean Orvieto and its caves

So much of what one finds now of the Etruscans is underground, but not because that's where it was originally meant to be. The tombs at the base of the cliff were gradually buried as people built their houses on top of the mesa and dumped earth and detritus over the edge of the cliff. Some of the Etruscan structures, such as cisterns for rainwater (for that was how they got their water here on top of the plateau where there are no springs), and conduits bringing that water from one house to another, were underground. The Etruscans were masters of hydraulics and we could well learn from them today. This subterranean "realm" is a cultural and anthropological treasure trove waiting to be discovered by the adventurous soul.

Orvieto has been compared to a sort of Swiss cheese, riddled with tunnels and wine cellars, harboring who knows what kinds of stories. Still now occasionally the paving will give way, with a car parked above falling into a void. The Cantina Foresi on the Piazza del Duomo, where you can also get a cappuccino or a prosecco, will be happy to show you their wine cellars. Or you can, and should, take a tour of Orvieto Underground, letting yourself be transported back to prehistoric times when the whole valley was covered by the sea. It is only relatively recently that the caves and cavities of all sorts hidden in the dark under the streets of Orvieto have been opened to the public. It all dates back to over twenty-five years ago, when a group of speleologists or cavers ventured into some of the grottos on the south side of the cliff, overlooking the valley below. One of the cavers was my son, the archaeologist of the group, employed in surveying what lay beneath the streets of Orvieto, a project that was part of the "saving of the jewel" of Orvieto, after a massive landslide threatened that side of the cliff. A German newspaper had warned its readers that they had better hurry and come to see the Cathedral before it slid down into the valley.

What is now a park leading down to the caves was originally simply a dirt path in the midst of weeds. Highlights of these guided tours are a sixteenth-century olive press, pozzolana quarries, columbaria or dovecotes, and tunnels of all sorts. Pozzolana, a volcanic slag, had been discovered by the Romans, who used it to make hydraulic cement that hardens under water. It is thanks to pozzolana that so many of their structures are still standing. The Etruscans on the other hand built their walls in dry masonry. My son, the archaeologist of the group, enlisted me as a guide since I also knew German and of course English. Now the organization employs guides in various languages so you have your choice of Italian, English, German, French, and more. It's really a journey back in time. The secret to any guided tour is enthusiasm. Same for your own approach. When I was training some of the guides, I told them they were to talk as if it was all an exciting new discovery they had just made and couldn't wait to pass on their information. So if you do take the tour, be sure to let us know if the guide lived up to your expectations.

Once I was telling a group of first graders that during the war people used the caves as air raid shelters. Another story – the war. One little boy piped up, *"but how did the planes get down here?"* Then there was the time I had a group of Americans on a reward trip to Europe. They had spent a few days in Rome and their guide told us not to worry about making the tour too long since they hadn't even taken up the option of a visit to the Sistine Chapel. I'm sure none of them even knew what that was. So I told myself, hmm. I'll make this interesting for them. And I started off as if I were telling my children a fairy tale. I captured their attention for the full hour. My son was silently observing on the sidelines, trying his best to muffle his laughter. He told me afterwards I practically had dinosaurs walking through the caves.

While a structure built above ground can be destroyed and change the aspect of the city above – the world below is tenaciously resistant. It can be filled in, walled up, isolated, but "deleted" only by digging it up, creating something even larger, a curious form of retroverted destruction. This is why the underground spaces constitute the key to an interpretation of the layout of the city that once was, that changed and grew and eventually imploded. The cantinas under the center of Piazza Duomo tell us of the houses of the canons, torn down to make way for the construction of the Cathedral. They, in turn, had been built on pre-existing Etruscan structures. Contemporary reports tell us that *"The parish church of San Costanzo was destroyed, and S. Maria Prisca, which was once an ancient Temple dedicated to idols made of beautiful and white marble".* The many-layered city.

Caves have always fascinated us. But there is also something frightening about a dark hole, about the unknown. One wants to enter, but one is afraid of entering. Who knows what strange beings live there? Even Leonardo da Vinci felt this primordial awe and terror. *"Drawn by my desire to know... I came to the entrance of a large cave: before which, amazed and ignorant of such a thing, I bent down and resting my left hand on my knee, I shaded my eyes with my right and leaned here and there to see if I could discern anything; immediately, two things rose in me: fear and desire; fear of this threatening dark grotto, desire to see if there was some marvelous thing inside"* (Leonardo da Vinci, Arundel Codex, London, 263, f. 155).

Ripa Medici, Porta Romana and valley fog - Picture by Erika Bizzarri

I wonder where the cave he was drawn to was. Could it have been Orvieto where we walk the streets, unaware of the tunnels and grottos of all sorts under our feet? A marvelous example is the cellar, privately owned and a veritable rabbit warren of passageways, under a house on Ripa Medici, on the way to the elevator that takes one to the principal parking lot. It was more than a simple wine cellar, for there are rooms with windows in the face of the cliff as well as multiple levels. For five years now archaeologists have been investigating several of these rooms. Truckloads of earth have been removed and still the strata continue to disclose signs of human presence. The deeper one goes, the further back in time one goes.

Not only that, but one of the chambers has turned out to be in the curious shape of a pyramid. A pyramidal space. It subsequently turned out that there were many other cavities of this shape, apparently the result of quarrying for tufa. A reporter who interviewed my son by phone got things rather mixed up and the headlines the next day in Italian newspapers, quickly taken up by Russian, French, English, and German papers, echoed what the Italian thought was a scoop: the first Etruscan pyramid! My son's answer was that pretty soon someone would say it was a launching pad for aliens from Mars! While we do go back in time, in this case even to the Bronze Age, finds also bear witness to more recent times. Analyses have also been done on the bones and earth, so that we now know what the diet of those who lived here was, and what plants were growing.

Traces of a kiln and broken ceramic fragments and discards bear witness to the revival of medieval pottery ware in 1922. Known as the Vascellari workshop, it was directed by the Orvieto artist and ceramist Ilario Ciaurro, and if you're lucky you can still find pieces signed by him in some of the antique shops. I am always fascinated by the discarded pots, where the glaze ran, or where three or more pieces stuck together make works that would hold their own in any show of modern art. The kiln also seems to have been used to make the over life-size "Etruscan" warriors (foto) sold around 1915 to the Metropolitan Museum in New York by the Riccardi brothers, antique dealers with a shop on Piazza Duomo. We now know they were famous forgers, in particular of Etruscan "antiquities", and it took some convincing to get Gisela Richter, renowned authority on ancient sculpture, to admit that they were fakes and not "one of the most dramatic things in the museum" as she asserted when they were acquired. When I first came to Orvieto, one of the Riccardi brothers still had an antique store on Piazza Duomo, now occupied by the Barberani wine shop. The caves on Ripa Medici subsequently became a carpenter's workshop and a friend of mine, a lawyer, remembers studying down there as a boy in the 1930s while his father invented novel ways of hooking up his woodworking machinery.

Once more, let us follow Calvino's advice as we try to decipher this many-layered city where you peel away one layer and, like an onion, there is always another one underneath. A good example is the church of Sant'Andrea, with Etruscan structures overlaid by Early Christian walls and mosaic paving, creating a labyrinth of their own right beneath the thirteenth-century floor you are blithely walking on.

If you go down the steps on your right when you enter, that's where you end up. Back with the Etruscans, who are never far away in Orvieto, even though the city was razed when they were defeated by the Romans. Signs of their presence are there if you know where to look -- a grave marker incorporated into the wall of a house, a glimpse of steps leading down to a room cut into the tufa (protected by glass) in a trattoria. Or in a church, like Sant'Andrea.

Coat of arms - the city's visiting card – Calvino, Invisible Cities – or perhaps not if you know how to read the clues

Aside from its logo, be it a cathedral or a fortress, the visiting card of a city is often its coat of arms. That of Orvieto, cross, eagle, lion and goose, gives you clues to what was involved in its past. The red cross in a white field is a symbol of loyalty of the Commune to the Guelphs (papacy), conceded to the City by Pope Hadrian IV in 1157. The black eagle with a gold crown refers to the rule of the Romans. The gold lambel, a heraldry charge, with five pendants was added to the eagle's neck when Charles of Anjou (d. 1285) gave Orvieto the title of "city" after he had been crowned king of the Kingdom of Sicily by Pope Clement IV in the then cathedral of Orvieto (date 1266). The lion in a red field holds a silver sword with his right paw and the keys of Saint Peter in his left, referring to the Florentine lion, and the historical alliance between the two cities. The keys, with the motto *fortis et fidelis* are a concession of Pope Hadrian IV in view of the long loyalty of Orvieto to the papacy. The goose, with one claw raised on a stone, brings to mind the legendary geese of the Campidoglio who, with their honking, saved Rome from an enemy attack.

Zaira, one of the author Italo Calvino's *Invisible Cities*, might almost have been Orvieto. It is almost too easy to paraphrase his description of this imagined city: *Zaira/Orvieto as it is today should contain all the city's past. The city, however, does not tell its past, but contains it like the lines of a hand, written in the corners of the streets, the gratings of the windows, the hidden courtyards, the television antennae, the protruding stones on either side of windows, every segment marked in turn with scratches, indentations, scrolls.*

Orvieto/Zaira, city of high bastions. I could tell you how many steps rise up in the courtyards, and the degree of the curves of a portico, and what kind of terracotta tiles cover the roofs; but I already know this would be the same as telling you nothing. The city does not consist of this, but of relationships between the measurements of its space and the events of its past: the height of a lamppost and the distance from the ground of a hanged usurper's swaying feet; the line strung from one lamppost to the one across from it and the festoons that decorate the course of the queen's nuptial procession; the height of that wall and the leap of the adulterer who climbed over it at dawn; the tilt of a guttering and a cat's progress along it as he slips into the same window; the firing range of a cannon which has suddenly appeared down in the valley. (Calvino, Italo, *Invisible Cities*, published in English 1974).

As we wander through the town, we can see signs of its past everywhere: the grooves in the tufa walls left by swaying carts that just barely managed to squeeze through the narrow streets, the low wall at the edge of the cliff, over which more than one have leaped to their death. A time-worn door, paint flaking off, half open, reveals tufa steps moving down into what is now a storeroom for firewood and building materials. In its previous life it was a pantry for prosciutto and cheeses.

Morning cappuccino, people and dogs

While we're talking about food, before continuing perhaps it's time for our morning cappuccino. You've been in Orvieto several days by now. You've become a regular at one of the cafes and have discovered the delights of sitting outside (this is presuming you're here in summer or before the chill autumn winds and rain set in) and watching the people go by. It's fun to try and identify the nationalities. Once it used to be by how many cameras they had hanging around their necks. But now they all, and I mean all, have their selfie sticks. The picturesque doorway or the Cathedral itself seem simply to be backdrops for a portrait saying: *I was here*. However, even if it is no longer summer or even autumn, and you have wrapped your scarf twice around your neck, there are people to be observed, outside or in. Some visitors have dogs as well as children in tow, but often the dogs belong to the

Italian townsfolk. They say the Italians aren't having as many children as they once did, but they seem to make up for it by "adopting" dogs – and you can set your watch by them as they pass. There's M with his white poodle. He is always nattily accoutered and never without his white straw fedora, stopping to talk to every other person he meets. There's R the dog psychologist with her own small spotted dog, who doesn't stray too far even though he is free to investigate whatever comes his way, while she walks two or three or even four other larger dogs on leashes. There's C, one of the women who own a restaurant down on the Corso. Her dog is big and shorthaired, part Irish setter and part Labrador, who strains at the leash. When you meet her she's probably on her way home after taking him on a long walk on the ring road that circles the city halfway down the cliff.

The benches in the piazza, or under the portico of the church, are mostly occupied by the men, who, depending on the weather, may also congregate in the cafes. They are all getting along in years (perhaps I shouldn't say so since I am undoubtedly older than most of them) and canes are ubiquitous. The women seem to have a coffee klatch of their own, generally in the afternoon. Mornings they are probably preparing dinner. Which reminds me of a wonderful story of an encounter I made at Vulci, another fascinating Etruscan site. It is a great example of typical Tuscan (although in this case we are in Lazio and not Tuscany) humor.

It goes back to November of several years ago. My cousin Tommy and I decided to go see the Etruscan exhibit in Vulci, about an hour from Orvieto. We parked by the forbidding fortress, rising darkly over the plain, and walked around to where the breath-taking hump-backed bridge spans a sheer rock chasm. Tommy went up ahead to a small half-hidden door. The only other people in sight at the parking lot had told him, yes, the museum was open. You just had to push the door to get in. I stopped to see what the little elderly man who was just setting up his postcard and guidebook booth had to offer. Since there wasn't another soul in sight, I struck up a conversation, just to be friendly. *"Guess you don't get many people at this time of year"* I remarked. *"Nah. I come here every day anyway just to get out of the house, to get away from my wife."* *"Well, I guess your wife is happy too, not to have you hanging around the house all day."* "If I were to be born again – not likely – I would become a friar. Wives are for the birds." "You have any children?" "Oh yes. Children are fine – young ones are fine as long as they're little – like lambs, they're great till they're four months old and then" – he made a motion as if to slit their throats – *"then you roast them."* "Oh well, have a good day." I then went on to push open the small wooden door and investigate the Etruscan innards of the fortress. When we left he was just closing down and we wished him buon pranzo as he took off for home... for dinner and his wife.

Orvieto has its goodly share of expats, and they will get together either in the morning, after market, for a cappuccino, or in the afternoon for their aperitif, at which point they may even flout Italian customs and have another cappuccino. If, however, you have opted for a prosecco or a Campari soda, that slightly bitter red aperitif, don't forget that if you're served anything with alcohol in it, the law says you also have to be given some sort of snack. Depending on where you are, it might be just potato chips and peanuts. Cafes like Montanucci's will add tiny pizzas or local tidbits that might almost be enough for supper.

Aside from the tourists who have decided to take a load off their feet, one can't help but notice some of the more eccentric habitués as they wander by, particularly in summer. I could tell you more stories here, but maybe I should respect their privacy and just let you look. There's the tall slender mysterious woman who seems to have stepped out of a gathering of the Bloomsbury group, pale and dressed in pastel colors, always wearing a wide-brimmed hat as if she were afraid of the sun, and with long skirts down to her ankles. She can be seen wandering up the Corso, or at some of the theater representations in the medieval quarter. Did find out later she was Russian and spends part of her time in Orvieto and part in Moscow. There's one lovely lady who has created her own particular persona. She is unmistakable for her voluminous skirts that could have come straight out of Gone with the Wind, where damask curtains were used to make Scarlett O'Hara a gown. Frequently with a fox fur draped around her neck or shoulders, she ambles along the Corso or sips an aperitif with her dapper but rather silent companion. A recent new addition are the Nigerians, who appear around ten and then vanish at one. Some have tribal scars on their cheeks, and most will hold out a cap, addressing you as mamma, hoping you'll give them some change. I generally have a euro ready for the first one I encounter. When the next one stops me, all I have to say is *"Ho già dato"*. *"I've already given"*. For from what I gather, they are a community and their takes all go into a single kitty. Walking the Corso, the main drag, you know summer's here when you seek the shade. Winter sneaks up on you with a wind that makes it almost impossible to cross Piazza del Duomo, and where you're always grateful for the sun.

No matter what the weather, the Orvietani must still have their coffee, read the paper, and discuss the state of the world. *"Oh yes"*, one of them once told me. *"My wife and I have divided our responsibilities. She decides on family affairs and I take over the important ones."* *"Like what?"* I asked for an example. *"Well she decides on what schools to send the children to, on the household finances, on the mortgage, and things like that." "And you?"* I asked. *"Oh, the important things, like the city government, and whether we should support the African states, and whether the taxes should be lowered."* Of the various self appointed guides haunting Piazza della Repubblica and del Duomo, there's one who I've been told is well versed in architecture and can be taken seriously. Most Italians do seem to have a good knowledge of their art and history. If you would be happier without their company, just say determinately *"Va via! Chiamo i carabinieri!"* and they will disappear like snow on a summer's day.

The people who are – and were

Orvieto without its long- or short-term inhabitants would not be Orvieto. They are the ones you look for every day and who give you a sense of belonging. You may not remember their names, but you know them. Take, for instance, the lady who cleans the escalator and elevator in the parking lot of Porta Romana (remember that doesn't mean it is a Roman gate but simply that this is the road that leads to Rome – but don't they all?). Once when I asked her if the escalator stairs were running, her answer came in pure Orvieto dialect. *"Nun so' signo', nun ci so' ita"*, where *"ita"* means *"andata"*, or gone, and comes straight from the Latin *ire*. Now if I hadn't been living in Orvieto all those years, I wouldn't have had the slightest idea that she was saying: *"Don't know, ma'am, haven't gone myself"*.

Typical of small towns are the bulletin boards posted throughout the city. Italian towns don't generally have their local newspapers, although the national edition may have a page dealing with local events. These bulletin boards replace them, either with posters on upcoming concerts or sales, or most often death notices. "You haven't ended up as a notice on the wall" is one way of saying you haven't joined the crowd of those who were. Glancing at the boards as you pass is how you keep up with what happens, and of checking to see when and where the funeral is. Since the ages of the dear departed are also generally given, one can't but help thinking that they were younger or older than we are. A few days go by, other notices are pasted over the old ones, the paper starts to peel off, and the memory of those who have left this world begins to fade. It occurs to me that there should also be a bulletin board with births.

On market day keep your eye out for the man with a hawk nose, painfully skinny arms, and a floppy hat pulled down low, as he transports boxes of chicory or artichokes, when they are in season, to the various restaurants. He could be mistaken for an Etruscan demon of the underworld.

One can be misled though. I thought the man who sells all kinds of honey must have Etruscan genes, for his profile was identical to that of the Etruscan reclining on the cover of his sarcophagus, in the Faina Museum. But when I asked, he said his family came from Genoa. Oh, well. That wonderful dignified gentleman with a white beard and cane – twin to the terracotta head of a man fingering his beard in the Faina Museum – whom you used to find sitting on a bench on the Corso or Via del Duomo every morning, probably did have Etruscan ancestors, though. His family is from Orvieto, generations back. For almost fifty years he was the Constable in the Corpus Domini procession, carrying a plumed helmet and wearing a magnificent full cloak.

The constable was one of the most important figures in those times, second in command only to the Lord. The months preceding the procession, he would let his beard grow. Visitors in the know used to wait for him to go by, cameras at the ready. There have been others in his role, but the procession is not the same without him.

It's easy to lose track of the celebrations of saints and political figures and holidays. Since my parish was that of Sant'Andrea, I was more aware of the role the church played in the neighborhood. Often, in passing, I might find elegantly dressed ladies (if they also wore large hats, of the type worn to royal weddings, it meant they were from the UK) and men in suits and ties expectantly waiting for the bride to arrive in a vintage car. Enveloped in her voluminous skirts, she would regally climb the steps to the church. Or there might be a somber crowd gathered around a hearse, waiting to take one of their members to a final resting place. While I am not what you would call a believer, I did have my sons get their first communion in Sant'Andrea, mostly because that was what their schoolmates were doing.

Sergio Riccetti - Photo by Erika Bizzarri

Italian holidays – the Miracle of 1264

Orvieto, and Italy in general, is full of holidays. Aside from the local saint days, carnival is celebrated here too, a sort of preliminary to Lent. While Venice is famous for its fantastic masks and Viareggio for its floats, in Orvieto you're most likely to be pelted with what in English we call confetti, but what the Italians call coriandoli. Confetti in Italian are the sugar-coated almonds and you run the risk of losing an eye if these are thrown at you. Confetti originate I believe in Sulmona where they may also be with a chocolate heart, and are distributed in uneven numbers for baptisms and weddings, generally in a multiple of the number 5 symbolizing the 5 good wishes for newly-weds of health, prosperity, happiness, fertility and longevity. Carnival for the children is dressing up as fairy godmother or batman and throwing handfuls of confetti/coriandoli at unsuspecting passersby. One year it was flour, which made your coat rather messy. When my children were small, Zorro was all the rage and I made them Zorro capes in black satin. Of all the holidays, Easter though is particularly impressive. The evening before, what in Italian is called *"vigilia"* or simply *"eve"*, the inside of the church looms dark, filling with worshippers just before midnight. Then suddenly the bells toll and the church is ablaze with light as the candles of the Resurrection are lit.

Easter mass the next day is preceded by the traditional Easter breakfast including various salamis, fried lamb cutlets, hard-boiled eggs, Orvieto Easter bread with pieces of cheese in it, or the sweet bread with a hint of cinnamon and rosolio, a rose liqueur. Curiously enough, the Orvietani call it *"pizza di Pasqua"*, whereas what we generally would call pizza is termed *"torta"* or cake. The cinnamon and rosolio version is to be nibbled on at the end of the meal, accompanied by a piece of chocolate from an enormous chocolate egg containing a surprise in the form of a plastic key ring or something more valuable. I have had chocolate eggs made to order for my grandchildren, with special surprises, such as a piece of jewelry or a memento. All this takes place about ten o'clock in the morning, to be followed by an Easter dinner of countless courses at the other grandmother's house. Despite the fact that he is a vegetarian, my son has me make coratella, lamb innards cooked with wine, rosemary, garlic and chili pepper. It's tradition, he says. As are the colored eggs which, true to my American upbringing, I dye in robin-egg blue and red for the occasion.

May and June. Easter, Pentecost, *Corpus Domini*. If you've timed your trip properly, you'll be here for one or the other of these events, although it is particularly *Corpus Domini* that is an unforgettable immersion in Orvieto's past.

The Palombella (palomba is Italian for dove), or Pentecost, comes fifty days after Easter and ten days before *Corpus Domini*. The descent of the Holy Spirit is symbolized by sending a pigeon, stand-in for a dove, along a wire that reaches from the church of San Francesco, at the other end of Via Maitani, to the Cathedral. The dove used to be tied to a rayed metal circle but after animal lovers threatened to boycott the event, it is now enclosed in a sort of space capsule. Even that, however, has aroused their ire. A few days before Pentecost, a baldachin housing figures of the Apostles and the Virgin Mary is set up on the steps of the Cathedral. As noon, on what you may be more familiar with as Whitsunday, approaches, the band plays as the crowd mills around the square. They are all keeping an eye on the balcony

Palombella - Picture by Erika Bizzarri

of the palazzo across the way, waiting for the bishop to wave a white kerchief as the clock strikes twelve. The sound of firecrackers exploding tells you that the dove has started on its flight from the church of San Francesco to the Cathedral. In less than five minutes it has arrived at its destination and lights go on over the heads of the apostles, symbolizing the arrival of the Holy Spirit and the gift of tongues. The fire truck parked off to one side – just in case – moves off as the cathedral workers climb up to retrieve the bird and then, holding it aloft, take it to the bishop.

You are particularly lucky if you can get hold of a piece of the red ribbon fluttering from the bird. I would love to get a photo of the hands stretched up in their attempt as it goes by. The dove (or pigeon) is then traditionally given to a recently married couple, who are supposed to see to its well-being for the rest of its life. At least it doesn't go into the soup pot!

If the dove's flight goes well, say the farmers, it's a good sign for crops.

My husband once wondered, rather irreligiously, what would happen if someone substituted a crow for the dove! Then there was the time a few years ago when the door of the capsule clicked open on arrival and the bird flew out onto a roof. It hopped around on the red tiles, bobbing its head and refusing to be captured. This was interpreted by some as a sign that the Holy Spirit was displeased with those who had "retired" the much-loved bishop to a monastery, despite the protests of the people.

Then ten days later comes *Corpus Domini.* One Thursday years ago (it used to be on Thursday but visitors beware for it is now on Sunday, although Thursday evening there is a small procession circling the Cathedral), I decided to see what the early mass was like, and after waking up to the peal of bells, took off for the Cathedral. It was still night and the empty streets were engulfed in darkness with my footsteps echoing on the cobblestones. At first it was only me, but then a nun in her dark habit and white-winged headdress materialized from the shadows. Soon, like a river gathering force, other early risers flowed in on their way to the Cathedral, where the tall doors were flung wide open.

The procession of *Corpus Domini* with its profound religious meaning and pageantry is in a sense synonymous with Orvieto. It all goes back to what is known as the Miracle of Bolsena. It was the year 1264 and Pope Urban IV, who was residing in Orvieto, was having problems with the heretical movement embodied by the Patarines (a part of Orvieto is still known by that name), who declared that the transformation of the bread and wine of the mass into the body and blood of Christ was purely symbolic. Orvieto seems to have been a hotbed of Catharism, the heretical movement that had seeped down from southern France and northern Italy, and to whose ideas the Patarines adhered. The pope had even sent a magistrate, Pietro Parenzo, to Orvieto. He was to see to the laws and administer justice, and convince the heretical Patarines to change their ideas. His methods may have been too drastic, for he did not go over well with the Orvietani, and what happened to him is shown in a fresco in the Signorelli chapel. He ended up with an axe stuck in his head – thus making him a saint. I suppose that's because he died for the faith.

One might say then that the Miracle of Bolsena was made to order, was an answer to the pope's prayers as well as to those of Peter of Prague, who had doubted. For tradition has it that as Peter was saying mass in Bolsena, the bread and wine were really transformed into the body and blood of Christ. Urban IV now had tangible proof of the real presence of Christ in the sacrifice of the sacrament of the Eucharist. He thus officially declared the solemn church feast day of *Corpus Christi (Corpus Domini)*. Thomas Aquinas, who was teaching in the church of San Domenico at the time, wrote the liturgy for this solemnity.

Every year the city dons its most gorgeous medieval and Renaissance costumes, and 400 representatives of the nobles and the guilds and professions parade through the streets following the altar cloth in its silver reliquary. The costumes have all been made to order, with handwoven brocaded gold-thread textiles from Florence, and bespoke shoes and armor. Lords and magistrates. Trumpeters and drummers. Knights and pages. The ladies have a day all their own, for in the 14th and 15th century they could not have been included in such a procession. As the constable, the people's captain, the magistrates and judges, the lords from the surrounding countryside, and the representatives of the guilds slowly walk in procession, following the silver reliquary with the cloth, you forget that they are really the shopkeeper, the artisan, the waiter who yesterday served you your pasta. They have been transformed, even for a few hours.

You might wonder why this blood-stained altar cloth is in Orvieto and not in Bolsena where the miracle took place – a good question. First of all the pope was here and it was considered tangible proof of what is known as transubstantiation. And secondly, a relic of whatever type means that pilgrims flock to the town, with all the monetary advantages involved, from lodgings and food, to the sale of souvenirs.

On their way to the Holy City, Rome, pilgrims often passed through Orvieto along what is known as the Via Francigena and the Via Teutonica. Even now, whether or not you are a pilgrim, you can enter the Cathedral by the side door to visit the chapel. I like to think of groups making the trip rather like Chaucer's pilgrims in the *Canterbury Tales*.

Some, such as the German Abbot von Stade, who traveled along the Via Romea Germanica in 1236, have left us detailed descriptions of their journeys and the distances covered every day.

Orvieto, free Commune, Monaldeschi and Filippeschi

In the twelfth century Orvieto was what is known as a free Commune, in which power was in the hands of the district lords, bankers, merchants and those practicing the liberal arts. The *populo* consisted of the growing middle classes who could not become members of the guilds and were initially excluded from political activity. They did however elect their representatives who made the laws. It was none other than the separation of powers, considered a modern theory. The people originally met in an outer space, a sort of loggia, which then eventually became the City Hall. The Podestà who put the laws into effect was the executive power and he had an office that was isolated so he would not be influenced by local politics and was elected for six months or perhaps a year. He was eventually replaced in Orvieto by a real government around the end of the thirteenth century when the Comune became a real state. It was the Signori Sette, representing the Guilds, who saw to the public works, such as streets. The Capitano del Popolo, or People's Captain, represented the judicial power, was military commander, and was also elected for a year.

The presence of the Church with popes and their retinues also played an important part in the economy of Orvieto, which was incorporated into the State of the Church in 1449 and then the Kingdom of Italy in 1860. The conglomerations of city-states in what eventually became Italy seem always to have been warring with each other, frequently changing sides. Power and the ownership of the territory were what mattered in these struggles between the Guelph papal factions, the Monaldeschi in the case of Orvieto, and the imperial factions, the Ghibellines or Filippeschi. There is an inscription on the Torre del Moro at the beginning of Via della Costituente (that short street that takes you from the Corso to Piazza del Popolo, skirting the Palazzo dei Sette) citing the famous verses of Dante's Divine Comedy, where he puts the rival families of Orvieto on a par with the Montagues and Capulets of Verona, of Romeo and Juliet fame. In 1313 the Filippeschi were finally exiled. Human beings however will always be human beings and, once the Monaldeschi took over, the various branches started bickering among themselves. They were identified by their coats of arms – the Monaldeschi della Vipera, della Cervara, del Cane, dell'Aquila (Viper, Stag, Dog, Eagle). Paul II succeeded in imposing peace only by having Pietro Antonio della Vipera marry Giovanna della Cervara (1465). In those days marriages had nothing to do with love, but were business and political contracts.

The countryside around Orvieto is dotted with castles of the ruling lords, identifiable by the type of crenellations: rectangular shaped merlons for the papal Guelphs, and swallowtail merlons for the imperial Ghibelline fortifications. Most of the castles still extant belonged to the Monaldeschi, who had finally succeeded in ousting the Ghibelline Filippeschi. A chronicler tells us that in 1313 there was fighting in the streets of Orvieto for three days and at the end there were 4000 dead. An exaggeration? But perhaps not. The Filippeschi were exiled and their tower houses torn down. I rather imagine the rubble went to the highest bidder. I sometimes think of this when wandering the streets at night, returning to the car park after a lecture or dinner. There would have been no street lights and I would have had torchbearers and armed men accompanying me, for one never knew who was lurking around the corner. In any case no lady would have been out alone at this time of night.

In the thirteenth and fourteenth centuries Orvieto was a bustling construction site. Streets were being paved, palazzi were being built, and the remains of towers, some of which had left casualties behind, were being cleared away. The only remaining tower of the many that once characterized Orvieto seen from afar is the one known as Polidori, which we'll pass later. I have an idea that things got done faster then than now, where in Amatrice, more than a year since the 2016 earthquake razed the town, it is still nothing but piles of rubble.

Over the years it was not only the Filippeschi towers that collapsed. Monaldeschi towers might also fall by themselves. The cause might have been faulty building or earthquakes, or possibly simply that the building materials deteriorated as time passed. A matter of fate? As the narrator says in Baricco's *The Legend of the Pianist on the Ocean*, one never knows. Maybe it's all been decided ahead. Say, on May 12th, the tower will fall. Twenty years from now, the tower will fall. And it does.

Church of Sant'Andrea, papal politics, Pranzo di Ferragosto

A good place from which to begin to get an idea of the more recent (say around the twelfth century) history of Orvieto is the church of Sant'Andrea. It was on the steps of Sant'Andrea that the nobles of the surrounding castles swore allegiance to the Commune. It was from here that Pope Innocent III declared the Fourth Crusade (1201), that Pope Honorius III consecrated Pierre d'Artoise as king of Jerusalem, and that Martin IV was declared pope in the presence of Charles of Anjou and his glittering retinue - all events listed in Latin on a plaque under the portico. Martin IV (died 1285) was the last of the French popes to hold court in Rome. The subsequent French popes beginning with Clement V, moved the papal court to Avignon, where they remained till 1376. It was of course all a question of politics, where you either sided with the papal party, the Guelphs, or with the imperial Hohenstaufen Germans. The various city-states were in a state of almost permanent warfare, the one siding against or with the other, changing sides as seemed most to its advantage. Florence and Orvieto were continuously battling Siena, the Guelphs against the Ghibellines and the Hohenstaufen troops of Manfred, for the dominion of Tuscany. A particularly bloody episode took place in 1260 in Montaperti where the Orvieto troops had taken refuge in the castle and when that fell to the Ghibellines, they were massacred.

 The church of Sant'Andrea also has a role in one of the most important holidays for Italians, the 15th of August, known as *ferragosto*, or *ferie d'agosto*, August vacation, when all Italians seem to be at the beach, and tourists take over the empty cities. On the eve of the 14th, the feast of the Assumption, when Mary was assumed body and soul into heavenly glory, her statue is taken from the Cathedral to the church of Sant'Andrea. The religious feast of the Assumption, alias *ferragosto*, in Sant'Andrea in Orvieto dates to 1338 when Mary was proclaimed patron of the city. On the fifteen, again at noon, a solemn procession takes her back home with the carriers racing up the steps of the Cathedral.

While it is basically a religious holiday, most Italians simply think of ferragosto as the beginning or end of the summer vacation. There's a great Italian movie regarding ferragosto and trying to put together a dinner for a gaggle of old ladies. The problem is that at *ferragosto* everything closes. The English title for the film *Pranzo di Ferragosto* is *Mid-August Lunch*, which doesn't at all put across the idea of unexpectedly having to prepare a real, traditional six-course dinner on a day that is a holiday and everything is closed. It is a film worth seeing. It gives you an idea of what Rome in mid-August is like, and the problems of what to do with your elderly mother, or aunt when you want to go away on vacation. Many of these problems are now solved by caretakers or *badanti*, from Albania, Moldavia, Romania, in any case Eastern Europe. Home care of elderly relatives has become a real problem in Italy, with both parents working and practically a complete lack of places to "park" the increasingly older population. To think that once it was just those grandparents who helped out, seeing to the young ones!

Before entering, let's look at the church of Sant'Andrea and its piazza from outside again. The story that entrances people most deals with the *pietra della vergogna*, the stone of shame. There were equivalents in many towns, where debtors would be exhibited and publicly shamed. A particularly famous one was in Florence, in the so-called straw market in the Loggia del Porcellino, where a stone in the paving still marks the site. In Orvieto there was once one right in the square, in front of the church of Sant'Andrea. I can imagine the poor man (or maybe not so poor – he should have known better) who cheated on the price of the fabric he was selling and got caught at it. Or who couldn't pay his debts. He was publicly disgraced, his pants dropped and his naked butt, and all the rest, exhibited to the taunts of the crowd. It was the disgrace more than the actual physical treatment that would haunt him for the rest of his life. This seems to have been a fairly common custom in the towns of the time and more than one have their "stone of shame"

Then there is the twelve-sided tower. There's another one like it at the abbey across the valley from the town. The one was inspired by the other – but which one? The tower of Sant'Andrea was rebuilt in the 1920s restorations. While there had originally been a tower here, reconstruction based itself on the tower of the abbey of SS. Severo and Martirio across the valley, dating to the eleventh century. While the tower serves as a sort of linchpin between church and city hall, religion and politics, apparently at times each side seems to be passing the buck to the other regarding its upkeep.

Some complain about the fact that there is a florist's shop under the portico. True, porticos were originally meant to shelter pilgrims, but nowadays most pilgrims just come for the day before returning to their buses. So I see nothing wrong with its present use. The different kinds of flowers testify to the change of seasons, or the holidays like Christmas. One day I was showing a couple from New York around Orvieto – she was interested mostly in finding a linen tablecloth large enough for their banquet table, in other words shopping, and I doubt whether she was interested in anything else. As we passed the florist under the portico of Sant'Andrea, a hearse in the street was being loaded with wreaths. The husband excitedly wanted to know more, and the florist obligingly took him to his workshop where other wreaths were being assembled. Turned out the gentleman was a mortician in New York – which may also explain why he and his wife were so well off and had a private chauffeur – and perhaps why she needed an enormous tablecloth.

Inside, the church is inviting and cool on a hot summer day. Over on the left wall the fresco tells the sad story of Saint Julian the Hospitaller who thought his wife was cheating on him. He returned unexpectedly from a trip and finding two people asleep in their marital bed, killed them both, only to discover that they were his parents who had come to visit. As in all the churches, there are lovely little details to be discovered. There's St. Christopher carrying the Christ Child on his shoulders, with a fish swimming in the river he is wading. Those geometric inlays on the pulpit do look familiar if you've already been up to the Cathedral. Even if I've told you there are other things to see, you couldn't have resisted the temptation to get a glimpse of what Orvieto is most famous for. These inlays here are quite like the mosaics on the columns of the façade of the cathedral, but they are Early Christian, and the panels come from another church.

Century upon century. St. Julian 1400, St. Christopher 1300. The pulpit, 10th century. And if you go down the steps on your right when you enter, you are in an even earlier layer, or several layers. Early Christian with its mosaic pavement, Etruscan walls and conduits. No, we're not done with the Etruscans yet. That young archaeologist standing by the steps, a colleague of my son's, is waiting to explain it all to you. His English is quite good, too, as he shows you a whole series of cisterns and how these masters in the art of hydraulics solved the problem of ensuring a supply of water up here on top of the cliff.

Epiphany, manger scenes, Befana, an Italian Christmas

Sant'Andrea, both the square and the tower, are often at the center of events. From political rallies, to protests of all kinds, to special fairs. Since Orvieto is also the headquarters of Cittàslow, the Slow Cities movement and its concept of leisurely living, weekends are often devoted to stands where one can sample wine, cheeses, and other local delicacies. At Christmas an enormous Christmas tree is set up in the midst of the square and at five o'clock in the afternoon on January 6th, Epiphany or the Twelfth Day of Christmas, the *Befana*, a legendary old lady riding a broomstick, slides down a cord from the tower. She also makes the rounds of houses in the villages, delivering garlic and charcoal (actually black rock candy) to the "bad" children and oranges and candy to the "good" ones. The story is that when the Three Kings passed by, she was too busy cleaning house to go with them to take gifts to the child Jesus. After they had left, she changed her mind and tried to catch up with them, but never did, and now wanders around leaving gifts for good (and bad) children. It can get to be rather confusing, especially when various traditions come into play. Santa Claus? The Christ Child? The Befana? A Catholic friend of mine whose husband was Jewish had tried to keep both Christian and Jewish traditions, but it turned out to be too much in the way of presents for their daughter, who was brought up Jewish.

There's a saying that the Befana takes all the holidays away. And she truly does, for afterwards the children go back to school and the Christmas trees are undressed and put outside to hopefully recover and put on new growth for the next year. For Christmas trees in Italy are sold with their roots.

Nativity scenes, known as *presepe*, are much more an Italian tradition, and not only in Umbria. They were supposedly begun by Saint Francis and sometimes represent whole villages with shoemakers hammering on their shoes and washerwomen beating their laundry. If you're in Orvieto for Christmas, perhaps also waiting to take part in Umbria Jazz Winter, you can make the rounds and visit them all for they are open to the public. There are small ones with homemade figurines, artistic ones, the one in the Pozzo della Cava with its life-size moving mannequins reenacting some aspect of the story, and then some one-off events where real people take the parts of the Holy Family and the Magi.

It took me a while to get used to the Italian Christmas for mine had always reflected my family's German heritage. The only Christian aspect I knew was a Christmas pageant at Bradford Junior College in Massachusetts where my father taught. At home my sister and I used to take turns being the angel Gabriel and Mary. My first Italian Christmas dates to 1955, when I was just an American freezing her fingers off in Rome. It was the first time I had heard of what they call *geloni* or chilblains. "Just get a salve from the pharmacy." my landlady told me as she brought me a raw egg to suck from the chickens she kept on her rooftop (and this was in the center of Rome) and a glass of brandy. But back to Christmas. At this time of year there are bagpipe players wandering around in Piazza Navona – shepherds from the Abruzzi region with baggy sheepskin trousers – playing just about the only Italian Christmas song I ever heard – *tu scendi dalle stelle – from starry skies descending* - although Silent Night and White Christmas were also very popular. There were manger, or nativity, scenes in some of the piazzas but not much in the way of Christmas trees.

If you want to have a traditional Christmas Eve dinner, you had better think ahead. The fishmongers (guess that's what they call them in the UK) will be sold out, for the locals in the know will have put in their orders weeks ago and will be waiting in lines to pick up their clams, mussels, cod, fish from the lake of Bolsena, but also eels. Yes, eels. It is said the popes were particularly fond of eels and had them sent from Bolsena. But then the popes also said ducks were OK to eat on fast days because they ate fish and therefore were not considered meat. One year my in-laws in Perugia were given an eel – alive – which they put in the refrigerator. When the maid opened the door to get some milk, out it jumped, slithering over the kitchen floor until some brave soul managed to capture it. I discovered that there is a lot of talk online of a seven-fish dinner but most of the Italians I know never heard of it. After *crostini* or canapés, (my favorite memory is of bread toasted on a wood-burning stove, then spread with butter and anchovy paste), our first course would be pasta and *ceci* (chickpeas), followed by the fish course with perhaps fried cardoons known as "*gobbi*". There's a traditional dessert I've never tried however, considered "peasant" fare. Some kind of short pasta, seasoned with grated chocolate, walnuts, cinnamon and sugar. Makes me think of our rice puddings.

So even though I'm not Italian, and not Catholic, I follow the traditions, and we have a fish dinner Christmas Eve, which also works out fine since some of the participants are fish-eating vegetarians.

Palomba, City Hall

One of the busiest pharmacies is right next to the tower. Via Garibaldi begins on the other side of the arch. A slight detour on the little street to the left, under the arch, takes you to one of the oldest family-run trattorias in town, the Palomba, where at lunch you're likely to find the mayor and town councilors as well as savvy tourists who have reserved in advance. Just tell Giampiero you're a friend of Erika's and you'll be welcomed with open arms. The Palomba is known for its *ombrichelli*, the hand-rolled spaghetti made of nothing but flour and water, over which Giampiero's lovely daughter grates an astonishingly generous amount of truffles, right before your eyes. An invention of theirs is the pasta named after Don Marcello, the marvelous priest of Sant'Andrea known for roaring from one country parish to another on a Harley Davidson, who had his own vineyard and who loved to eat, but who has now left us for, we hope, a better world. You might also want to try the tagliatelle with a traditional tomato sauce with chicken innards. Main courses include of course pigeon or *palomba*, a beef filet with an unexpectedly delectable nettle sauce, or wild boar stew.

I would sometimes take my granddaughter to lunch there, and even at ten she knew exactly what she wanted. In the back room one of the tables is set on a glass panel over steps going down into the rock. This was once the entrance to the wine cellar. Occasionally, surprised by this empty space beneath their feet, clients request to have their table changed to more "secure" seating.

Back on Via Garibaldi, the entrance to the City Hall leads up what I would call ramps, possibly so horses could more easily navigate them. They are rather like the "steps" in St. Patrick's Well, meant for mules or donkeys. No pun intended here. The official municipal rooms contain paintings of cardinals and bishops who are part of the history of Orvieto, with frescoes on the ceiling depicting the small towns that owed allegiance to Orvieto. In the mayor's office are gifts from the various sister cities (Bethlehem; Givors; Maebashi; Aiken SC; Seinajoki; Kercem Malta; Avignon) and the typewriter on which the German commander of Orvieto in 1944 wrote his request to have Orvieto designated an open city, thus saving it from wartime destruction (more on this later). There are also examples of Orvieto lace and ceramics.

If, as you pass by outside, you see flowers on either side of the street entrance, pause and wait for the bride and groom to appear after the civil ceremony in which the mayor reads them their wedding vows. If rice is scattered over the cobblestones, then the bridal couple is already off to their banquet, and the pigeons can have a feast. I remember that when Mario and I were married in Perugia, in far-off 1957, it had been quite hectic. We arrived at the city hall – and no one knew where to go. Finally the red tapestry-walled room was found tucked away in a corridor, and a small round-faced man with a tri-color sash around his middle (who knows if he was the mayor) read us the rules and regulations. I'm sure I hesitated a moment before saying, "Yes". They seemed much too "man is lord and master" to me, much too medieval Italian, and I felt it quite unfair that no one had warned me.

I believe things are a bit simpler now. Nor does it have to be the mayor officiating. At times a special friend or relative may stand in for him, as when my younger son and his wife were married by his godmother, wearing the mayor's tri-color sash of authority.

Via Garibaldi, partisans and painters, master masons and nuns

Across the street is the hotel named after the legendary Aquila Bianca or White Eagle. Ermanno Monaldeschi was training his falcons when a white eagle appeared from nowhere. Ermanno's gyrfalcon won the battle, and the eagle was found dead in a ravine, to be stuffed and join other trophies in the Monaldeschi palace in Piazza del Duomo. A white eagle was thereafter depicted in the Monaldeschi coat of arms. Further down, on the left side of Via Garibaldi, is Federico the shoemaker, who married one of the American study-abroad students.

Across from him is Svetlana, who has a specialty wine shop. She grew up in Serbia, in Sid, in the province of Vojvodina. Her father was in the military in close contact with Tito, and she remembers being there when the military leaders of the various non-allied countries had their meetings. Gaddafi, she told me, was 24 when she saw him.

At the curve is the palazzo where seven "partisans" were tried and convicted. Some were in hiding to avoid conscription in the Fascist armed forces, and were anti-fascist. The Germans, in command in Orvieto, were against the death sentence but the Italian Fascists overrode them and they were executed as an "exemplary" punishment. Known as the massacre of Camorena, there's a plaque in honor of the victims outside the building. Livio Orazio Valentini, Orvieto's finest contemporary artist, also made a painting of the massacre. It now hangs in the Governor's Room in the Palazzo dei Sette.

At this point you can either go left or right. Left takes you along Via Garibaldi, to a point where cars come around what seems to be a blind corner. True the mayor is trying to eliminate traffic in Orvieto, but you can't keep all cars out. Now cross over to the street straight ahead of you, after checking the cars, and watch out not to bang your head on the imposing window surrounds, particularly on Palazzo Saracinelli in Via Alberici. If you could get inside you would find yourselves in a fairytale labyrinth of wooden figures – Etruscan warriors, lion, horses, birds of all kinds. This is where the Michelangeli family store their historical wooden figures, and the more modern workshop is up above, only a fraction of the size of these storerooms. A bit further up, where the street is so narrow cars have to wait if a pedestrian is going by, there is a piazza with a small modest door leading to the convent of the Buon Gesù, of the Poor Claires. Another story if you're looking for one. As all buildings in Orvieto, the convent too needed repair work every so often, which was seen to by a charming master mason who had lost his wife three years earlier. Since the Poor Claires are a cloistered order, meaning they can't have contacts with the outside world, the mother superior had received a special dispensation so she could discuss things with the master mason. Maybe you can figure out for yourself what eventually happened. The nuns said their prayers seven times each day, and one morning Anna, the mother superior, was nowhere to be found. A small tidy sort of woman, she had simply left the convent and showed up on the doorstep of the master mason.

Try to put yourself in her shoes (or habit) and picture her asking God for guidance. It was a scandal of course and made all the local and even national papers. The bans were published and after the required waiting time they were married by the communist mayor, with two anti-clerical communist witnesses. I used to see them walking up the Corso, hand in hand, and now one can still encounter her occasionally since he has passed away.

But the convent has more to offer than a story straight out of Boccaccio. If you go by on a Sunday, stop in and listen to the sisters singing. I said it was a cloistered order, so that generally the nuns would participate in the services in a room behind the altar with only a grate through which they could hear the priest officiating. Here though the choir has been moved into the aisle, separated by a railing.

San Lorenzo, catering school, words

Further up there's another church which has a story all its own. I told you that Orvieto is full of stories, hidden at times behind those tufa walls. Well, San Lorenzo dei Arari originally dates back to the eleventh century, but was rebuilt where it is now in the late thirteenth because the nearby Franciscan friars complained that the hymns and prayers of San Lorenzo bothered them. And I guess the Franciscans were those in command. There he is, Saint Laurence, on high on the left wall, saving the souls from limbo, giving alms and being martyred. There certainly were different ways of torturing these early Christians. Laurence was roasted on a grill. *"I'm done on this side, you can turn me over now."* And he doesn't actually seem to be suffering all that much. So we have the name of the church, San Lorenzo. But what about the word Arari? Ara means altar and the Christian mensa or altar stone rests on an ancient Etruscan altar. On Sundays San Lorenzo is now orthodox and an iconostasis or screen with icons separating the nave from the altar hides the apse. On high in the conch the figure of the enthroned Christ looms up, accompanied by the Virgin and various saints. There are also panels with frowning Orthodox saints on the left hand wall by an altar before which the Orthodox priests in their heavy gold damask apparel perform mass, unless they are hidden behind the iconostasis.

Across from the church is the *scuola alberghiera* or catering school. Years ago, shortly after my husband died, I was given a temporary appointment there, teaching English to the 15-16 year-old boys who at the time were learning a trade. There was one lesson I'll never forget. We had gotten to the possessive case and for the life of me I can't imagine what the author if the textbook had in mind, for the secondary meaning in English is the same as in Italian. "I play with my balls". "You play with your balls". We got through that lesson in record time. There are countless hurdles or opportunities for misunderstanding in using a language you did not grow up with. How often tourists want to order peach tea (*tè alla pesca*) at the bar and end up ordering fish tea (*tè al pesce*). But the waitress is quite used to that. Then you might think you were telling your hosts how marvelous the dinner was when you say it was *tremendo*, unaware that in Italian the word means terrible, or horrible, and not wonderful or stupendous.

Continuing up there's another piazza, with the rather bare façade of the church of San Francesco. Orvieto does seem to have a plethora of churches and convents, in part because it was on the pilgrim route to Rome, the Via Francigena. In the late twelfth century the most important religious orders began finding sites inside the city and not just outside where they already had the Abbey of Saints Severus and Martyrius and the Convent of the Trinity. They ended up by forming a sort of loop of convents around the top of the cliff, which might be another good way of making the rounds.

Library and Marino Moretti, back to Piazza Ranieri

While San Francesco had its convent and was one of the most important churches, what is not to be missed in our itinerary is the library, a remodeling of the Franciscan convent that had been turned into a barracks and a school. While we'll have more to say about the library itself later, right now what interests us is the children's section and the sort of amphitheater outside where the concrete benches have tiles of the seasons by the ceramic artist Marino Moretti. I'd go there just to see those. Opening hours are a problem though, because of lack of personnel, or let us say money.

Bench with ceramic tiles - Artist: Marino Moretti

We could continue down Via Maitani here, but it might be best at this point to return to Svetlana's where the street turns off Via Garibaldi and continues under an arch, where most cars politely wait for us to move on. An artist's studio is followed by Alberto's court of miracles, a world of gnomes, castles and fairies in terracotta. He is undoubtedly a real Etruscan for his family has been in Orvieto for ages. One would never guess, but he had studied at the art academy, as well as three years of architecture at the university. Nothing to give him a job though, so he worked as a waiter. One day he saw an empty shop for rent, grabbed the chance, bought a kiln, and even though he had never worked with clay, began making his gnomes and towered castles. That was ten years ago and he is still at it. A few doors down is the exit (or entrance) of the escalator that leads to the underground parking lot. This by the way is the best place to park – in the shade in summer. Out of the rain, or even snow, in winter. Be sure to take your entrance ticket with you for when you leave you pay on the upper floor, which takes you to the escalator or elevator. If you opt for the former, be sure to note on your right, as you come up, stone sections of the medieval aqueduct that look rather like mint lifesaver candies. Fitted into each other, lead pipes were inserted in the holes. As you continue through the tufa rock on which the city stands, near the top, look up at the remains of an Etruscan cistern and a medieval tunnel, intersected by the excavation works. They are all parts of the city that was. In the square, Piazza Ranieri, the gas station and garage once here have gone the way of the remains of one of the fountains where the local women went in the sixteenth century to draw water. The convent of San Lodovico now offers hospitality to passing pilgrims and those who just want to sit and enjoy the peaceful garden where wisteria has almost completely covered a tree at one side. The mother superior is an energetic figure who almost single-handedly turned the convent, where young girls studying to be teachers used to live in typical eighteenth-century dormitories, into a welcoming b&b. She could tell you stories too, about their underground caves and the frescoes in what was once the original church.

At the fork of three roads is the Mezza Luna, a great trattoria, famous for its carbonara made with *guanciale*, or pork jowl, egg and pecorino. Better reserve ahead, and don't think you can order a half portion of their spaghetti carbonara. Averino, your host, never heard of such a thing, although he will let you share. A few years ago to celebrate the 30th birthday of his carbonara, he made a hundred portions for enthusiasts who had gathered at the Palazzo del Gusto.

Taking the street to our left, we once more head to the edge of the cliff and the Grotte del Funaro, and the Palazzo del Gusto now renamed Palazzo del Vino. The battlemented piazza in front overlooks Via della Cava with its houses piled one on top of the other against the cliff. It's tempting to stop and just look out over the city and the pattern of fields and vineyards below.

Overlook of Via della Cava - Photo by Alfredo Casuso

Piazza della Repubblica, City Hall, Ippolito Scalza

Best though to return to Piazza della Repubblica (also commonly known as Piazza Sant'Andrea or Piazza del Comune) before moving on to the church of San Giovenale.

But wait. Since we're passing through Piazza della Repubblica once more, maybe we could see if Ippolito Scalza is hanging around. One does have to take advantage of what comes one's way. There he is, on his way up to the Cathedral, a tall handsome figure with a beard.

"Ser Ippolito, could you tell us something about what you did here, please? We're always slightly puzzled by the fact that the façade of the town hall just stops at a certain point."

"Try my best, but just a few words so you won't be bored. It was the mid 1570s. We had it all planned out, in a finely balanced design, but it is never easy to adapt a building or façade to earlier medieval structures. See that second arch from the right, framed by double columns? That was supposed to be the main entrance, the center of the façade. And you'll note that the slight slope of the piazza has been compensated for by the high bases. When you look at architecture, you always have to ask yourself how and why. It also helps to know who and what came before me, but I'll tell you more about that when we go up to the Cathedral, which was, you might say, my life's work."

Before we have a chance to ask him why the façade of the town hall was never finished, he's disappeared along Via Garibaldi. Come to think of it, wonder what the street was called in his time? Perhaps they never got around to finishing the façade simply because the money had run out – typical of projects in modern Orvieto as well, for when is a municipal budget not always in the red?

Bar Montanucci and the Italian espresso; Gualverio Michelangeli

Since lunchtime generally doesn't begin till twelve thirty or one, and we have been wandering around all morning, it probably is best to sit down for half an hour or so and collect our thoughts while savoring another cappuccino and pastry. Or an aperitivo. No better place than Montanucci's café, which first opened over a hundred years ago It's one of the hangouts for regulars in the morning where they read a newspaper while waiting for Nadia or Natasha to bring them their pastry. No, you're not seeing double. These lovely young women are twins, originally from Moldavia. I have fond memories of Rosina, the mother of Reno Montanucci, who was the owner and one of the city's leading figures, sitting in a chair keeping an eye on customers and occasionally offering a cup of coffee to older acquaintances, rather to the chagrin of her son who was much more of a businessman and was one of Orvieto's standard bearers until his sudden death at the end of 2018. We still seem to feel his presence, sitting behind the cash register. "No, no, you pay afterwards. Just look over the pastries, choose what you like and tell the girl behind the counter that you would like a cappuccino or an Americano. Or sit down and the waitress will come and take your order. Hospitality is my password. You know this coffee bar has been here for a hundred years! When I was in grade school, I was known as the bar kid. My mother used to sit in that chair over there and keep track of the comings and goings. I really hope to plant a rose garden at San Giovenale in her honor. So go ahead and decide what you want for breakfast."

If you do have a sweet tooth, try the croissant with chocolate cream, filled to overflowing. I like the vanilla cream and jam combination best. Many pastries are on top of the glass cases and you can help yourself. Reno trusts you, and rarely has that trust been betrayed. Why not try the maritozzi con panna? I used to get these sweet buns, split open and filled with whipped cream, for my children on their way to school. Although come to think of it, most often my children had the traditional Italian children's breakfast of milk with barley "coffee" and bread broken into it. Just as for a snack they might later have a slice of bread, passed under the faucet and then sprinkled with sugar, or rubbed with a cut tomato, a sprinkling of salt, and olive oil. How much healthier in those days!

Talking about the Italian espresso, Bruno Bozzetto did a hilarious take on it in his cartoons on Europe versus Italy, and not only coffee. You can find these on the web. How do you want your coffee? Plain espresso. Lungo. Corto. Corretto (with a dash of liquorice-flavored sambuca and a coffee bean on top or grappa), macchiato (spotted) with milk, and now they even have "Americano", which means in a large cup. One of my first impressions of Italy had to do with coffee. It was 1955 and I had arrived in Florence the night before. The pensione was right on the Arno, and on the other side of the river there were still signs of the destruction of WW II. Even the bridge across the Arno was makeshift, a temporary wooden structure, replacing Ponte Santa Trinita. It was around eight o'clock when I walked out the pensione door and crossed the river into a rather frightening melee of people and cars. I was terrified, as traffic seemed to take off in all directions, obeying only the policeman who stood calmly in the midst, gracefully motioning the cars to stop or go. The crowd eddied in and out of the coffee bars, drinking their coffee standing up. How odd I thought. Just a couple of gulps of coffee, maybe with milk and with a croissant, and that was breakfast. Quite a difference from what I had been used to coming from my relatives in Germany!

The Montanucci premises are unique, for if you look around at the wooden decorations on high and in the back room, you'll discover prancing horses, facades of houses with wooden tile roofs, figures peeking down from windows, tiny feet walking up a ladder all by themselves, sundry birds and animals, as well as three large giraffes at the back near the stairs leading to the outside terrace. They are all the work of Gualverio Michelangeli, whose father and grandfather were already making furniture in Orvieto before he was born. Gualverio prided himself on being an artisan and refused to call himself an artist. Once you feel you can continue your exploration of Orvieto, a bit further up, on the right, is Via Michelangeli, where his daughters now continue the family business. Passersby can rest on the bench that has a fanciful cow and its calves as a backrest. The large wooden horses on either side of the street are the delight of young and old. I think it was Rick Steve who mounted one and then with a wry smile said they weren't all that comfortable, at least not for males.

A bit further on is the church of the SS. Apostoli, now used for exhibitions, to the left of which the lane is lined with large wooden "doorways" leading nowhere and a sort of dry pool with a gazebo, signs you're close to the Michelangeli workshop, once a theater, with old carpenter tools and model cutouts up high on the walls. Gualverio Michelangeli, who died young in 1986, was truly a magician, and his epitaph in the cemetery is particularly poignant.

"They will come and remember him
as a good wizard
few were as adroit as he
in building dreams
fragments of sun
of joy
within the solid porous walls
of Orvieto."

Erika's shop: crafts and artisans

Perhaps this is as good a place as any to tell you about my shop. It was all thanks to Gualverio and the fact that my job in Rome had come to an end. It was 1967. No one could have predicted that Mario would die suddenly the following year, and that it would take two years for my pension to come through. It was thanks to the shop, and help from our many friends, that my two small children and I managed to continue to stay in Orvieto.

Gualverio Michelangeli, that "magician" who made layered wooden creatures to sell in his shop, thought it would be good to have an outlet right near the cathedral. We were sort of relatives, his grandfather a cousin of my husband's grandfather, and his children called me Zia Erika. My job in Rome had ended with the end of the alphabet and the McGraw Hill Encyclopedia of World Art no longer needed me to check up on spellings and facts and translate captions. Like Gualverio, I loved crafts. Real crafts, like hand-woven textiles and the rustic pottery splashed with green made and used in the countryside by the farmers. So we opened up the shop.

If you're in Piazza Duomo, look for the little street next to the tourist office. There's what they call a fountain at the entrance, once continuously spouting water. In summer when it was really hot, I would cool off by holding my wrists under the stream of cold water. Further up on the right are jasmine vines, now almost concealing a wrought-iron sign where if you look hard you can still make out the name: Erika. Further up the street, behind a wall, is an enormous magnolia tree, with unbelievable great waxy white blossoms in early summer. But back to the shop. There used to be another shop across the way, run by the wife of the custodian of the Cathedral, with excruciatingly kitsch wares, such as mugs with breasts, and still another smaller one just before Erika.

What I liked best about the shop were the contacts, scouring the countryside of Italy and the craft fairs, to find objects I could be proud of. There was a glass-blowing cooperative in Tuscany where I could go and load up the car with what they called seconds, vases that might be slightly off center, or had bubbles in them. Red was the most expensive color. They were beloved above all by the German tourists. Or there was Federico, the weaver in Prato, who made shawls and throws and if I needed a longer throw, all I had to do was tell him. He loved his work and said the great thing was that he could work on Sunday if he wanted to, and take off Monday, and no one could tell him what to do. When I went to pick up what he had done, he would ask my opinion on the colors. *"What do you think? Does this red go well with this orange?"* Sometimes then Gualverio would bring objects he had picked up in his travels through Italy. There were two five-foot high Sicilian puppets from Catania, figures in the *Saga of Orlando*, one rather fierce looking, a Moor or Saracen, and the other sweeter despite being dressed in armor and certainly Angelica. I'll never forget the young German couple who came into the shop and fell in love with the Moor. It was expensive and they came back I don't know how many times to look at it, finally cutting short their honeymoon to buy it. I wrapped it in a blanket and they set it regally in the back seat of their car. Hope no police stopped them on their way home, thinking it was a body. One also met interesting people. Many of those who came were delighted to find someone who spoke English, which not many did at the time. I remember a young man named Bob, in the military in Germany, who came in one day. He told me, not at all embarrassed, that he and his buddy had driven down from Heidelberg and at a certain point decided to leave the autostrada. There was a sign saying Firenze so they pulled off, got to the city, found a hotel and wandered around. It was only when it was time to go back to the hotel that Bob looked at his key. *Hey Joe. Do you know we're in Florence?* he exclaimed. Makes me wonder what they thought all those buildings and the river were. Since we were next to the hospital, which at the time was on Piazza Duomo, I frequently got called in when there were accidents with "stranieri" who spoke no Italian.

Now though, fifty years later, things have changed. The hospital is on a hill outside the city. The glass cooperative no longer exists. Federico has long since gone to make his shawls for angels. A host of other shops have sprung up in Orvieto and the rustic pitchers with green splashes are practically impossible to find. My potter from Ficulle, a word that in itself refers to clay, also made small clay whistles in the form of horses and carabinieri. His daughter got her education and became a teacher and he now lives in Orvieto and helps take care of his grandchildren. Times were not easy then, the shop had to be open seven days a week, but the exchange rate for the dollar was in my favor and I often had American students stay with me over the summer and help out. And I could, like Federico, close the shop, take my children and go swimming in Bolsena if I felt like it.

Piazza della Legna, dell'Erba, Loggia dei Mercanti, the Templars

From the Corso and Montanucci's and the Michelangelis, we really should continue our walk along Via Filippeschi. However there always seems to be a side street that beckons you to stray off the main path. That's part of the magic of Orvieto – you start going somewhere and before you know it you are somewhere else. There's a small piazza off to the right that seems to say, come look at me. Take a look at the windows of the palazzo too – they're called Guelph cross windows and are the only example in Orvieto. The name of the piazza, Piazza dell'Erba, tells you that this is where vegetables, or Erba, were sold. There's another piazza called Piazza della Legna, and that's where wood or *legna* was sold. The wellhead here was meant to be on the town hall terrace, although I still haven't quite figured out how. Until recently the printing press where Mario Bizzarri's guide to *Etruscan Orvieto* was published, and a wool and clothing shop where I remember seeing piles of wool that looked as if they has just been shorn – at least they weren't carded – waiting to be washed and stuffed back into mattresses as part of the spring cleaning before the priest came by to bless the house, were familiar to those passing by. They now exist only in my mind as do the laundry, where I took a damask tablecloth to be washed and then forgot about it, and the dairy where I got my fresh milk. Initially when I first moved to the cardinal's palace down the street, a milkman would come around mornings, tooting on his tin trumpet, and I would take my container down to have him fill it with milk. Probably wasn't pasteurized, but I wonder if I gave it a thought at the time or just boiled it. Giannino, who originally ran the dairy, then became the courier who took daily trips to Florence doing errands for whoever needed something not available in Orvieto. Before the era of the floppy disk and email, I would give Giannino the typewritten pages of my translations to be delivered to the Florentine publishing house and he would bring back whatever the next assignment was.

Leaving the piazza and crossing Via Filippeschi, no, we're not going down that street yet, another brief detour to Via Loggia dei Mercanti, where the town hall ends, won't take all that long. A few steps and our eye is caught by a striking Gothic arch that has something to do with the Sovereign Military Order of Malta, who replaced the Templars, suppressed in 1312. Most of us are acquainted with the Templars from novels and films, most recently Dan Brown's *The Da Vinci Code*. The local headquarters of this historic Christian military order was at Bardano, 6 km west of Orvieto, across from where the Neri Cantina is now on high, a splendid site well worth a visit. Not only were the Templars intent on freeing Jerusalem from the Muslims, but they had also built up an imposing financial network as bankers, thanks to the fact that their sites were on the principal communication routes, and could transfer money from one city, one country, to another. Here in the city they had a bank, a church (dedicated to St. Matthew, the tax-collector) and a residence, subsequently taken over by the Knights of Saint John of Jerusalem, knights Hospitallers of Malta. The legendary Knights Templar were one of the reasons the popes were in Orvieto.

A bit further on down this street, on the right is Torre Polidori, the only tower still standing of the many that once distinguished Orvieto. Legend has it that this was where the knight Polidori kept his beautiful wife prisoner. On summer nights, Charlie's Pizza in the shadow of the tower is filled with young people and families. Don't be surprised if small children are still wandering around at eleven at night, or perhaps even asleep at the table. They are part of family life and using baby sitters to put them to sleep early is unheard of. The former church of S. Maria del Carmine across the way was without a roof when I first came to Orvieto. and I used to pass it as I took my children to the kindergarten in San Lodovico. I must say they were not all that enthusiastic about the nuns and the teacher, who, according to my oldest son, spent most of the time at the mirror. However, I had no choice since I was the breadwinner for the family.

Palazzo del Gusto/Vino, wine tasting, American Thanksgiving

Sometimes people ask me if Orvieto has changed and I have to stop and think. It may seem it hasn't but then it really has. The Carmine, restored and now with a solid roof, is the site of theater and concert activities, with ghostly saints looking down from the fragmentary frescoes still visible inside. Apparently it is the only part of Orvieto that some unfortunate visitors experience. I went to a gospel concert there once, a group from Charleston. They had arrived at five, and had just enough time to rehearse before the concert, scheduled for six. They didn't even know what town they were in! They were to leave the next morning for, of all places, Bari, but I insisted they stop and at least get a view of the cathedral. Not sure who organizes tours of this sort, but they need a good shaking up.

Continuing past the Mezza Luna, that trattoria famous for its carbonara, we find ourselves right at the edge of the cliff with its marvelous view of the valley. The Grotte del Funaro (*funaro* means rope) is down around twenty steps into some of the caves under the city. Near a lookout window in the cliff wall there's a carding device and a wheel on which the hemp fibers were twisted into rope. Before being processed, the hemp stalks had to be macerated in ditches filled with water to separate the fibers. The smell of the rotting stalks would linger in the air for weeks. Indeed, old timers will still refer to Via Filippeschi as il Cordone, for this was where the ropes were then laid out.

Across from the restaurant is San Giovanni Evangelista, attached to the Palazzo del Gusto, now Palazzo del Vino. This is where the regional Enoteca, or wine library, is housed. During the year there are frequent wine-tasting events in its underground premises, where one would learn to distinguish between one vintage and another, and where young American students would be told that they were never to fill the glass to the top, but only about a quarter full. The row upon row of bottles that line the walls hold promises of summers of years past and the city once more has its many-layered stories to tell. Echoes of medieval times reverberate in the steep steps cut into the tufa and the ramp for the barrels over to one side, while the terracotta conduits half hidden under the floor take us back to the Etruscans.

Up above, the main entrance of the Palazzo del Vino opens onto a lovely Renaissance cloister, perfect in its mathematical harmony. The well in the center got its water from a cistern where the rainwater was collected and purified by passing through gravel. In summer, dinners were occasionally held in the courtyard, and the sky would turn red and gold as you were elucidated on whatever vineyard and whatever restaurant was being featured. Once, my dinner companions were a university professor and an architect, both of whom were Orvietani and known to be particularly fond of wine. It takes little to guess what the conversation was about. Sometimes though I had to help out foreign guests when their knowledge of Italian, but not of food!, left something to be desired.

One year Orvieto's sister city of Aiken, South Carolina, decided to offer the Orvietani a Thanksgiving dinner – even though it was only October. Missives went back and forth as to what the cooks from Aiken required – turkeys, sweet potatoes, and corn. When the delegation arrived, they were told the six turkeys were already there, and that they were without legs! Oh, my Lord! No drumsticks? Actually the young woman had translated the Italian *"senza zampe"* as "without legs", when *"zampa"*, the word for paw, also means foot when referring to a feathered creature. When it turned out that the turkeys did indeed have their drumsticks, but were without feet and heads, the Aikenites breathed a sigh of relief. Generally if you get a fowl at the butcher's, you get it all, heads and feet and innards. Years ago when I was preparing my first Thanksgiving dinner in the little town of Monterubiaglio I had had to order the turkey beforehand. Of course I meant a whole turkey to be properly dressed and roasted. When I went to pick it up, the butcher proudly showed me the bird and began to cut it up. Horrified I stopped him, probably much to his dismay, but then I found an ideal solution. I bought a chicken and skinned it, and a bit of plastic surgery on the lower part of the turkey breast kept the stuffing inside the cavity where it belonged.

My Aiken friends were also at a loss as to what to do with the ten bags of popcorn piled up by the kitchen door, for what they had requested was of course just plain corn. And sweet potatoes? We did manage to find some in the supermarket, but they were of the white kind. So making the most of what was available, we mixed them with orange pumpkin and lo and behold we had our sweet potatoes of the right color. The Orvietani honored this Thanksgiving dinner, gobbling everything up, surprised mostly when everything was brought to the table at once –- no first and second courses. They also did a double take when before the meal they were introduced to the southern custom of saying grace before the meal.

One year, some of my son's friends also learned what a thanksgiving dinner was like. Claudio showed up at the house one day and asked if I would prepare a turkey. "Sure. How big is it?" "25 kilos!" "*That's not a turkey, that's a dinosaur. That's over 50 pounds!*" Somehow I did manage to dress the bird, which one of the friends had raised in the country, but then the problem arose of where to cook it. Certainly not in my oven, it's barely large enough for a normal turkey. The answer was finally found when our butcher, who also roasted whole pigs, offered us his oven. The dinner was in a farmhouse at a long table in an ambience the pilgrims would have found, let's say, familiar. I had also made corn chowder, naturally with milk (with milk? But surprisingly the Italians liked it and even asked for seconds). Then when it came time for the *pièce de résistance* to enter, it was brought in on a sort of stretcher carried by four strong young men. Could well have been an Etruscan banquet. Except it certainly wouldn't have been a turkey.

The Pilgrims and the first thanksgiving probably might have had what we then came to call turkey, since Columbus thought he had reached the Indies, and that was what this indigenous American fowl came to be known as, referring to its supposed Turkish origin. Around Orvieto and Perugia a dialectal name for turkey is *dindi*, referring to India. And believe it or not, Italian turkeys speak a different language from American ones. We were once driving through the countryside, when my American friend said she knew how to talk to turkeys. Leaning out the car window, she began to call: *gobble, gobble, gobble*. The turkeys paid absolutely no attention. Then our Italian friend leaned out and said: *glu glu glu* and the turkeys answered right back.

Via Malabranca, Catherine de' Medici

To return to Via Filippeschi, which goes as far as Via della Cava and then becomes Via Malabranca. This is the quarter of San Giovenale, which is also still a real neighborhood. We'll head down the steep Via della Cava later, but first we'll continue on Via Malabranca (named after Ugolino Malabranca, who died in 1374). What we are actually headed for is the church of San Giovenale where, among other things, the tombstone of this Augustinian bishop of Rimini, carved with his life-size image, lies underfoot. Originally prelates or nobles were buried inside churches and the closer to the altar or some special saint or relic, the better their chance of getting to Paradise. Napoleon, however, thought otherwise, and emanated an edict in 1804 prohibiting burial within the city or convent walls. This was actually not a bad idea from the point of view of hygiene. After all most bodies decompose and if they remain intact, even after years, it supposedly means they are saints. Cemeteries thus began to be set up outside the city, for by 1809 the entire Italian peninsula was under French control (by which is meant Napoleon, of course, who had made his sister Elisa grand duchess of Tuscany). This is why you won't find any really old monumental tombs in Italian suburban cemeteries, unless of course you go back to the Etruscans. If you stay longer in Orvieto and enjoy being out in the open, the cemetery across from the city itself (begun in 1867), with its stands of cypresses, associated by poets and artists with the dead, would be an interesting place for a stroll, and the inmates would have a lot to tell you.

Continuing along Via Malabranca on your left, you are overlooking Via della Cava, where on one side the buildings are backed up to the cliff. The bell tower of San Giovanni Evangelista rises to the sky across the way on the other side of the dip of Via della Cava. Via Malabranca though is perhaps best known for the Filippeschi-Simoncelli-Petrangeli palazzo, to our right, where an enormous pine rises up behind a high garden wall. This was where Catherine de' Medici stopped in 1532 on her way to marry the future king of France, Henry II. She was still a child but must certainly have been mature for her years. Who would have thought that more than 50 years later this 14-year old, by then queen mother, would have been responsible for the horrendous massacre of the Calvinist Protestants or Huguenots. Indeed there are crowds waiting for her arrival now. Very likely she's tired, for to get up here her litter would have had to be carried up that steep Via della Cava.

"My lady, we hope your trip went well and that you had a favorable impression of Orvieto."

"How tiring trips of this sort are and certainly Orvieto and its cathedral look so out of the way. Of course I'm used to traveling since I've always been shuttled back and forth from one convent to another, mostly for my safety. I was only nine when that unfortunate sack of Rome happened. At present my uncle Clement VII, a Medici, and Francis I of France are working out the marriage agreement between me and Francis' brother, Henry of Orleans. Of course no one asked me if I wanted to marry him, but that is quite normal. Let's hope he is a gentle man. After all I'm only 14. I have, however, learned to put my foot down. I wonder what my favorite cook, whom I had sent on ahead, is preparing. Perhaps a savory tart with shallots or chickpea puree, a soup with herbs, small birds on spits or on a crust, perhaps with truffles, and since the lake of Bolsena is not far off, there might be a roast carp dressed in sugar and rose water. Certainly there will be fruit and quince and small cinnamon and honey cookies. All with the best of Orvieto wines, watered down a bit, of course."

Whatever else this cook prepared one can be sure there were no potatoes or tomatoes. But why? you say. Well, look at the date. America had only recently been discovered and exotic foods, like potatoes and tomatoes, corn and squash, had still not been accepted as "edible" foods.

An aside. I was once invited to a wedding in a village not far from Orvieto. We arrived in time for the reception at the home of the parents of the bride. Dressed in a fairy-tale gown that must have cost a fortune, she then walked through the streets of the town, accompanied by her relatives, on the way to the church. My husband explained that it was a way of showing the townsfolk that the bride's family had succeeded socially and financially. I hadn't realized at the time that the custom went back to Roman times when the authority of the *pater familias* over the whole family could not be questioned. In the Middle Ages, too, the bride would walk from her father's guardianship, to that of her husband's. No in-between. She was always subject to the male. Present law of course allows the couple to choose between shared or separate ownership, and if it isn't specified and one or the other want to sell, say, their car, the spouse also has to sign. The Etruscans were rather more advanced in this respect, for their women could own property and had rights of their own. While women of a certain rank in medieval and Renaissance Italy could also own property and inherit, they were still always under male tutelage. In leafing through sixteenth-century Roman archives, a friend of mine found a document where an heiress with considerable wealth of her own (she was her father's only heir as he had no sons) remarried after her husband died. Her second husband seems to have been a scoundrel and continually tried to get his hands on her money through various schemes. In order to disinherit him, she had to swear before 11 priests that he no longer had any rights to her property and then she named her eldest son her heir. While women could often manipulate their husbands in Italy and in the other European countries, in the early modern period under English common law, for instance, the legal identity of women still depended on the husband or father. Progress in that sense does seem to have been made.

If the tall wooden doors to the Filippeschi-Simoncelli-Petrangeli palazzo are even slightly ajar, go in. Or perhaps you can sneak through the entrance on the other side. Once more, thanks to the medieval windows and a Renaissance courtyard, you'll find yourself immersed in several centuries of history. The most recent owner was a close friend of my husband's and about the most absent-minded doctor one could imagine. He was known to show up at the hospital wearing two ties, for at the time a tie was mandatory when on duty. So just to be sure, he sometimes put one in his pocket to be pulled out as he was racing up the steps, oblivious to the fact that he might already be wearing one. He was highly respected in his profession, however. As was the norm, he began as a country doctor, and the story of his first delivery involving a farmer's family is hilarious. Driving through the hills, he frantically leafed through the manual, comforted by the fact that the midwife would also be present. Turned out it was her first delivery too! Not only that but after the child was born, he noted that there was something amiss. *"Maybe it's just the afterbirth,"* he ventured. Closer investigation revealed that it was . . . another baby! He and the midwife had just assisted at the birth of twins.

The palace he and his family lived in, and whose courtyard you are now admiring, had belonged to his grandfather, on whose death it had gone in part to his father, in part to his uncle. Since in Italy you can't disinherit your children, he had only had what is known as his legitimate share. Can you imagine how complicated it can get where an apartment may belong to as many as 16 heirs! One day he arrived home and nonchalantly announced that he had bought back the half of the palazzo previously inherited by his uncle. Not surprisingly, his wife was at a loss for words, for the whole palazzo was enormous and now included a private chapel, a ballroom with frescoes, as well as a tower and a labyrinth of cellars. Ten years after my archaeologist husband died, it was here in the small chapel that I married Adamo, my second husband.

Back on Via Malabranca, after a dozen steps or so, be sure to look up at the molding of the stringcourse, that decorative horizontal band separating the second-floor windows from the ground floor, on the palazzo across the way. I think I would have liked the bishop owner for, as you read in the inscription: *"Caravajal de Caravajal por comodidad desus amigos padron"* (Caravajal de Caravajal for the convenience of his friends master of the house). One gets an idea of a human being who valued his friends above all. In other words they were the ones his palazzo was for. It had originally been built in 1548 by an Orvietano, Cardinal Simoncelli, whose name still appears on some of the door surrounds and who seems to have been responsible for a considerable number of buildings in Orvieto and in the surrounding towns. This palazzo was subsequently modified by that extraordinarily friendly Bishop of Sovana.

Another extraordinary person lives in the palazzo next door. She's over ninety, but has lived life to the full. As a young girl she had to put her foot down to convince her father, a judge, that she wanted to study medicine at the university. How many women, 70 years ago, were even going to the university? Now retired and with a slew of nephews and nieces, although no children of her own, she still oversees the agricultural activities on the family lands in the area. She has traveled the world, always taking along some spaghetti for her much less adventurous husband. Her terrace is home to a marvelous collection of roses, and she knows each by name. It's always easy to find a gift for her. One can add either to her assemblage of around fifty teapots from all over the world, or find another lizard of some kind – glass, ceramic, wood – to accompany the many already perched on her mantel or peering out from under a table. There is something aristocratic about her, for she is a landowner and has a maid who keeps her house in order. Yet she still prides herself on mending her old sheets. She once told me

The Lady welcomes you - Photo by Thomas Gerish

that before she married, her future mother-in-law instructed her on how to starch and iron her husband's shirts. This nonagenarian but still youthful friend of mine is another of the secrets of Orvieto, hidden behind the façade of her palazzo. How many other living treasures could one discover if one had time and were good at asking questions!

Sant'Agostino and Mochi, Ippolito Scalza, San Giovenale

Past a few more palazzi, with a street on the left that goes down to connect with Via della Cava, and we end up in the large Piazza San Giovenale. The church of that name, one of Orvieto's gems, is on a small side street that runs off to the left. First though, since we're in the piazza let's go to the former church of Sant'Agostino over to the right, next to the tall glass façade of another church that had been turned into a restaurant, but has now been closed for years. At the ticket office in Sant'Agostino, (it's part of the Cathedral museum and the Carta Unica gives you access to this and various other venues) there's a large black-and-white photo of the cathedral before its unfortunate late nineteenth-century "modernization", when it was decided to return it to its "pristine condition", meaning removing any work that was later than the 17th century. Until recently this former church has been used as a temporary venue for the statues of the Apostles and patron saints that had once been part of the Cathedral accoutrement.

Since I wrote about Sant'Agostino in 2018, things have changed. It is still the place to go to see the giant photos of what the Cathedral looked like before it was deprived of its paintings, frescoes, and gilded altars, with the statues lining the nave. But in November of 2019, in a challenging undertaking, the Apostles and the patron saints of the city were returned to the Cathedral and set up on their original bases, with up-dated anti-seismic footings. They once more keep watch over the nave, their backs to the columns, urging you to go forward to the apse where two marble figures of the *Annunciation* flank the altar. Perhaps they are best commented on when we finally cross the threshold of the Cathedral.

Finally here we are, at the church of San Giovenale, which almost seems hidden at the very tip of the butte. Probably built on the site of a temple to Jove, the façade is quite simple and unprepossessing. The view, with Rocca Ripesena, that miniature Orvieto, rising up in the distance, makes up for it all, though. The bell tower, not quite in line with the main building, was built on the foundations of a lookout tower, from which whoever might be approaching from the north could be seen. Another sign of Orvieto's warring or defensive nature in the Middle Ages. Orvieto, the teller of tales. A sandstone bust of Giovenale or Juvenal is set into a half shell in the lunette over the door to the side entrance. Not much is known about the saint himself and his ghost is probably haunting the walls of Narni where he was bishop.

Inside, if you know where to look, there are signs of changes made when the church was extended in the late thirteenth century from its original early twelfth-century Romanesque forms to the Gothic, visible particularly in the vaulting. The English guidebook to San Giovenale has a scholarly and detailed analysis of this architectural development and its relationship to the political and stylistic choices of the time. I am particularly taken by the idea that one of the reasons for the large chancel, the space where the altar is located, in late thirteenth century churches was that hymns of praise and church plays could be performed there. Heaven with God, was in the apse, hell under the left arch, the terrestrial paradise in the chancel and under the right arch, while the world was in the lower part of the nave, with the public. If you are lucky, you can attend one of these performances where the citizens of the quarter take on the parts of the Apostles and God, with reference to the unusual tree of life with its complex iconography on the counter façade of the entrance wall.

San Giovenale, its walls and pillars covered with frescoes ranging from the 13th to the 15th century, can give you an idea of what once was. Sit quietly and perhaps you will hear the echo of a laud, praising the Creator or the Virgin Mary, for it is she one sees most often here as she presents us with a very serious little Jesus, a hieratic priestly figure. "*This is Jesus, my Son, the source of Salvation.*" He is not yet shown as a real baby, as in Gentile da Fabriano's fresco in the Cathedral, a couple of centuries later. You may also, with the aid of the English guidebook to the church, like to identify the scenes and the rather stern saints who have been looking out on the visitors, perhaps with only one eye, for centuries.

As I was translating the book I began wandering around the church hoping to meet some of the saints. Saint Leonard, for instance, was described as holding tongs or pincers. Finally a voice came from over to my left. "*Looking for me, are you? Not many people pay much attention to me, standing by myself and clutching some shackles, of the kind used for slaves. Yes, I know. They are often depicted as tongs or pincers. The sixth-century emperor Clovis granted me permission to free prisoners so that is how I am shown. Actually I was Frankish and my shrines sprang up along the pilgrimage routes.*"

It is really great fun to try and identify the various saints. Note that Saint Anthony Abbot has a tiny pig at his feet, and it is belted, of the kind still raised in Orvieto. The pig refers to the fact that pork fat was used in the cure of shingles or by the much more poetic name of "Saint Anthony's fire" and a bishop in France had given the Antonian monks permission to raise pigs for this purpose. What has always fascinated me most is the altar, where a slab of Byzantine interlace dating to the 9th century has been recycled. There's also a date in an inscription on other parts of the altar referring to a certain Abbot Guido, around 1170. At the corners, the capitals of the pilasters are sculptured with a dove, a griffin, a bishop or abbot and St. Michael Archangel overcoming Lucifer.

It's not only what we see, and try to understand, that lets us imagine what Orvieto was like in the fourteenth to sixteenth centuries. The parish books often provide surprising information that gives us an insight into details of the history of the city and the cathedral workshop. For instance, we know that there was a certain painter known as Arrigo Fiammingo (Flemish, in other words) involved in the decoration of the Cathedral in 1561. We also know that there was what might be called a resident colony of artists, especially from Flanders, in Orvieto. Remember that artisans from all over Europe had been employed in the construction of the Cathedral from the very beginning. And now we have one of the parish books in San Giovenale where the marriage of Arrigo Fiammingo with Donna Ortensia Sensati is registered. The date is 1576, and while Arrigo was no longer employed by the cathedral workshop, he evidently was living in Orvieto. I like to imagine their courtship. It's another example of foreigners coming to Orvieto and making it their home.

Via della Cava, the Well, the festivals

Retracing our steps back to those butcher and bakery shops, and keeping an eye out for cars coming down the Cordone as well as from a smaller street on our left, we start the steep descent along Via della Cava. No, the word cava has nothing to do with cave but is the Italian word for quarry and some of the tufa used in building was quarried here. Come to think of it, I haven't told you that tufa is basically a conglomeration of detritus laid down in the valley when the volcanoes around what then became lake Bolsena erupted, 370,000 years ago. The cliff of Orvieto, rising up over the plain after millennia of erosion, consists of tufa, with some travertine, a form of limestone, and with veins of pozzolana, a granular volcanic slag, which the Romans discovered was perfect for making cement.

There's a small church on your left, known as Madonna della Cava, and if you're there on February 3, the feast day of St. Blaise, you can have your throat blessed, with the priest crossing candles over your neck. Might do the trick, you never know. The local women also make *tortucce*, or thin fried bread rounds, for the various festas. They are delicious, whether you sprinkle them with salt or sugar.

Opposite on the right is the Pozzo della Cava, a deep well discovered accidentally in 1984 during renovation work of a restaurant. Originally Etruscan, it was enlarged in 1527, at about the time St. Patrick's well was being built, to supply water to this end of Orvieto. In 1646 it was closed, supposedly because five French officers guilty of molesting the local women had been thrown in. If you're wondering what the French were doing in Orvieto, they might have been members of the French army of the Franco-Spanish war (Thirty Years' War). The well and a whole warren of caves are now visible, together with much of the material found in the excavations, including a medieval kiln and discarded pieces of pottery. Other "rooms" include *butti*, or dump shafts, an Etruscan cistern and tunnel, and medieval wine cellars. At Christmas, Marco Sciarra, the enterprising young owner, has been creating pageants of biblical episodes with life-size figures. One year he put Mary and Gabriel halfway down in the well, and the speleo cavers had to lower her and themselves down on ropes to place her. The shop behind the coffee bar also has reproductions of medieval pottery and this is one of the best places to look. It seems that wherever one goes there are shops selling pottery, of all kinds of designs and colors. But the real Orvieto pottery is defined by the simplicity of its colors – basically very dark brown and green – and designs that go back to the fourteenth and fifteenth century. (foto medieval pottery)

Further down on Via della Cava, on the left, is a door that leads to the Etruscan wall, part of the only entrance to the city in Etruscan times. Again a chance discovery, further proof of how Orvieto holds more mysteries than one can imagine. Dating to the sixth century BC, it was discovered by my husband in 1965 when a medieval wall in a private home collapsed. It is a truly imposing structure, and one marvels at how the Etruscans succeeded in building it without mortar. It seems to confirm the description of what has been presumed to be Orvieto with only one approach to the city through the rocks. Procopius, the sixth-century Byzantine historian, in his passage on the war in which Justinian's general, Belisarius, besieges the Goths at "*Urbiventus*", describes it as follows: "*... the top level smooth but precipitous at the base ... Upon this hill men of old built the city and they neither placed walls around it nor constructed defenses of any kind since the place seemed to them to be impregnable by nature. For there is only one approach to the city through the rocks... (History of the Wars, VI:20).*

At the end of the street is the thirteenth-century city gate known as

Porta Maggiore, originally the main entrance to the city in medieval times and now one of the principal exits from the city and favorite refuge of pigeons. Again try to imagine what it was once like. I doubt, however, you would come up with as disastrous a picture as the one presented by Olave Potter in her A Little Pilgrimage in Italy (1911):

"The grim Porta Maggiore, where Boniface VIII in his twofold tiara, keeps watch from his niche above the gateway ... Through this gate hastened the Popes, fleeing from wrath to come, and in their footsteps we toiled up the steep street between the same houses of yellow volcanic tufa gone black. Through dark alleys we could see the gloomy depths of caves, hollowed out of the living rock behind them: in the low bassi the citizens of this broken city toiled silently, and outside their doors sat hooded owls on poles driven into the stony ground. There are some streets in Orvieto which look as though war had stalked through them only yesterday; as though the terror-stricken Ghibellines still cowered within doors, while the Monaldeschi rang bells in triumph, as they did on that fateful day in the year of grace 1312, when the Filippeschi had tried in vain to open the gate of the city to Henry VII of Luxemburg."

Perhaps by wandering along Via della Cava and one or two of the side alleys, particularly at night and ignoring the cars parked silently here and there, we can imagine ourselves back in the thirteenth century. Some of the houses still have their outside staircases, which led up to the living quarters, while the ground floor level was for the animals or used as a storeroom. Less than a hundred years ago when farmers came in on market day, they would hitch their donkeys up here before going into the city. Then upon returning, they would stop for a liter of wine and fried cod in one of the taverns along the street. The houses on the right as one descends are frequently backed up to the tufa cliff, which rises up sheer and offers a home to those ubiquitous pigeons. Someone once compared pigeons to human beings, proliferating everywhere and polluting their environment.

These dwellings, more than others, present us with an idea of the close relationship between the building and the space below. It was obligatory for each house to have a sort of dump shaft, known as *butto*, dug into the rock beneath the house. Dumping over the edge of the cliff would have raised the level of the ground and made it easier for what in Italian are known as "*malintenzionati*", prowlers or those who were ill-intentioned, to find their way into the city. When during restoration of the cellars, the butti are emptied, layer after layer of broken potsherds, or pottery fragments, come to light: the further down you go, the further back in time. There are cellars and tunnels under practically every Orvieto house, for with their constant humidity, temperature and ventilation they are ideally suited for conserving the mainstays of the family economy: prosciutto and sausages, cheese and wine. Steep steps cut into the tufa with inclined ramps on either side along which the barrels could be lowered led down to the lowest level where the wine was maturing in barrels. I've been in houses where the host would excuse himself, and go down into the cellar with a pitcher to get more wine.

Villages like Monterubiaglio still have an annual festival for the new wine, generally in December, when a large barrel of that year's grapes, sealed after picking in September, is brought into the village square, and the new wine spouts out of a hole bored in the side.

Sausages and bacon are grilled on charcoal fires as the locals and visitors down glasses of the new wine, to be finished that evening, before it takes on an acidic taste. When I lived there, we went to my husband's vineyard and grilled pork chops and bacon and drank the new wine, in a sort of round where the person whose turn it was had to drink up the glass. I remember in particular the singing that followed.

Bigonzo, celebrating new wine - Photo by Erika Bizzarri

Pope Boniface VIII

The niche at the top of that thirteenth-century city gate once held a statue of Pope Boniface VIII, while a second statue was set over Porta Postierla, bringing him accusations of idolatry. The originals of both are in the Faina Museum. Look, there he is, wearing a sumptuous cope and with that symbol of papal authority, the twofold tiara, on his head. He does look overweening, I might even say dour, as he disdainfully states that both spiritual and temporal power are under his jurisdiction. *"Every human creature is subject to the Roman pontiff. I am the Church. I am the Pope."* He came from a powerful Roman family, the Caetani, and I wonder if he hadn't been spoiled and always had his way. During his five months in Orvieto in 1297, his new papal palace, Palazzo Soliano, was under construction. While the Orvietani did elect him *Capitano del popolo* and *Podestà* in that year, he is often criticized for nepotism and greed. I suppose few politicians or popes can avoid accusations of this sort. Or perhaps only modern-day politicians?

Can't you see him as he declares "war" on the Ghibelline anti-papal Colonnas, and excommunicates them as well as Philip the Fair of France over a question of taxes? In the end though, he lost out, for Sciarra Colonna succeeded in capturing him in his palace in Anagni and is said to have slapped him with his gauntlet. Normally that would have ended up in a duel, but this was after all the pope. In the end it was the French who won out, and when the papal throne was left empty, it was the French who filled it with their allies and moved the papal court to Avignon. Boniface never fully recovered from his treatment by the Colonnas and after his death, a judicial investigation on the pope was held.

Palazzo Soliano is now part of the museum complex of the Opera del Duomo and the ground floor is devoted to the works of Emilio Greco, the sculptor of the doors of the cathedral, which were hung in 1970. He had donated a collection of his work to the city of Orvieto – with the stipulation that the entrance be on Piazza Duomo. After sundry suggestions and arguments, the ground floor of Palazzo Soliano was perhaps an obvious solution. The doors themselves, depicting the seven acts of mercy – are another story. When they were commissioned, the Opera del Duomo authorities had neglected to ask the Fine Arts commission in Rome what they thought about it. So when they were finished, Rome said: "*No way! The cathedral façade is already so busy it doesn't need doors of this sort.*" So for a couple of years the Greco doors were hung inside the church. Then I suppose the members of the Rome commission either retired or died, and once permission was given, they were hung – but guess what. They were hung at night so that when the Orvietani got up the next morning their cathedral had new bronze doors, whether they liked it or not.

Funicular, Cozza, Garibaldi, Jews and Muslims, St.Patrick's Well

I suppose some of you will have come by train or bus. Right across from the station is the funicular railway or cable car, which brings visitors up to the top of the mesa. It was designed by Adolfo Cozza, whose bust we'll later encounter at the foot of the external steps of Palazzo del Popolo. A sculptor, archeologist and inventor, he was born in Orvieto in 1848 and as a young man joined Giuseppe Garibaldi's volunteer soldiers, his "red shirts". And since we've brought up Garibaldi, maybe an explanation here would help. After all there is also a Via Garibaldi in Orvieto, as there is in practically every Italian town. This patriot and soldier of what is known as the Risorgimento, the movement that consolidated the individual Italian states into a single state of Italy, played an important part in taking back Sicily and Naples from the French Bourbon rulers, and contributed to the unification of Italy under the House of Savoy in 1861. By the way, he also championed women's emancipation, believed in racial equality, and favored the abolition of capital punishment. He stopped in Orvieto and spoke to the crowds from the palace where the local bank is now housed and is said to have toasted to the departure of his corps of volunteers or his "thousand" with Orvieto wine.

However we've gotten off the subject. So back to the funicular which was built in 1888, and used to run on water. The number of passengers would be relayed back and forth so that water could be added or subtracted from the car that hauled the other one up. It was still powered by this water system when I first came to Orvieto, was closed at the end of the 1970s to be completely revamped, and finally opened again in June of 1990, running on electricity with up-to-date video controls. Crossing over from the railroad station, in five minutes you'll be at the top of the plateau, in Piazza Cahen. I suppose you'll be asking who the Cahens were and what they had to do with Orvieto. You've also probably figured out that the name is a version of Cohen and that it is Jewish. Actually the Jews had been present in Orvieto, as they were throughout Umbria, since the thirteenth century. They were generally merchants, peddlers and loan bankers. They were in part later replaced as bankers by the Monte di Pietà, an institutional pawnbroker that provided loans at low interest, set up by religious organizations such as the Franciscans. As early as 1215 the Fourth Lateran Council had decreed that "Jews and Moslems shall dress in a way that will distinguish them from Christians". I never have figured out why human beings always have to have some "other" and can't live in peace. Curiously enough, I had never made a distinction between Jews and non-Jews even though when I moved to New York for my university studies, most of my friends turned out to be Jewish. You'll find Jews depicted in some of the frescoes in the cathedral, in particular a little boy wearing yellow, a color already associated with Jews in the fourteenth century. In Signorelli's fresco with the preaching of the Antichrist, there is a figure in the foreground identified as a Jew who is paying off a man or woman. An excursion to the small town of Pitigliano (an hour away) with its Jewish museum, and a Jewish quarter with a bakery and synagogue, might be something to plan when you want a change of scene.

In 1880, Edoardo Cahen, whose father was a wealthy banker of Antwerp, bought the Monaldeschi Castle of Torre Alfina. Edoardo provided funds for the struggle to achieve a united Italy and was given the title of marquis in 1885 by King Umberto I, which is I suppose why the square was named after him. With the promulgation of the racial laws in Italy, the last of the Cahens was forced to leave the country.

Many of the people we encounter in our story are not all that commendable, and with regards to Umberto, perhaps the less said about him the better.

Getting off the funicular, we could take a minibus to Piazza Duomo, but we want to see Orvieto and not just the Duomo. So let's walk. Here we have layers of history again, from the Etruscan temple of Belvedere, to the park on our right, which was a fortress, originally built for Cardinal Egidio Albornoz who conquered Orvieto in 1354 for the return of Innocent VI from Avignon and who was restoring papal authority in the States of the Church. The fortress was later torn down and rebuilt more than once. From the parapet one gets a good view of the three communication routes – the river, the railroad, the highway – running through the valley below.

The purpose of the well, which has always fascinated travelers, was linked to that of the fortress. As George Dennis said *"The two great lions [of Orvieto] are the Duomo, and the Well of San Patrizio"*. In 1527, after the sack of Rome by renegade troops of Charles V, Pope Clement VII, worried that his troops would have no water in case of siege, called in Antonio da San Gallo the Younger, who had already proved his worth.

"Of course, your holiness, the only answer is a well. A well that goes all the way down to the water table. Yes, I know it's 60 meters down and some think I am mad, but take my word for it, I can do it. I've already begun scouting around the base of the cliff to find the most likely springs. All you have to do is give me a free hand."

Clement VII, a Medici, does have a lot going for him. Not least that he knew his people. He was a patron of Raphael and Michelangelo among others, and in 1530 crowned Charles V Holy Roman Emperor (evidently he had made peace after the sack of Rome which wasn't really the fault of Charles V).

San Gallo was given the go ahead but the well wasn't finished until 10 years later, in 1537, when Clement had been dead for three years. It was quite an undertaking. Builder of palaces and military engineer, Antonio da San Gallo the Younger was already well known for his skill in solving problems. The idea was to dig through the rock down to the water table, 60 meters below. When the workmen came upon layers of clay and pozzolana, that friable material used in making cement, they had to build brick walls before going further. About halfway down they came upon a man-made cavity containing objects in bronze that has been interpreted as the remains of a Villanovan (pre-Etruscan) burial. The well is unique in that the stairs are in the form of a double spiral, so that mules could go down one ramp and come up the other, their barrels full of water, without getting in each other's way. Reminiscent of the DNA helix. Now just what does St. Patrick, who lived in the fifth century, have to do with the well that in the beginning was known simply as Il Pozzo della Rocca, or the well of the fortress?

The story of St. Patrick, and how he had a deep well that went down into Purgatory (in Ireland of course), became popular in Italy thanks to Jacobus da Varagine's thirteenth-century Golden Legend with its lives of the saints. You'll find the story of St. Patrick illustrated in a fourteenth-century fresco in Todi, another hill town about half an hour from Orvieto. It's a marvelous drive through canyons with the Tiber at the bottom flowing along into the dam of Corbara. Eventually our Orvieto well came to be identified with St. Patrick. You might also wonder who paid for the well. In part they were municipal funds, and in part subsidized by the Vatican. But the people too had to contribute their labor and transport the 30,000 bricks required. Finally in 1537 the well with 248 shallow steps or ramps was finished. It probably suffices to know that it's over 61 meters deep and that it has 72 windows. It's fun to see your friends across on the other side, as you go down and they come up.

Via Roma and military barracks, San Domenico and Arnolfo di Cambio

The left-hand street of the three leading to the city center from Piazza Cahen is Via Postierla, referring to a small entrance to the fortifications; the middle one is Corso Cavour, which is pedestrian; and the one on the right is Via Roma, where there's underground parking. What for Italy are modern buildings now cover what used to be fields and vineyards. Our old friends, the Etruscans, seem to have had a kiln here too, but since those large buildings on the right as we start walking up Via Roma are now on military ground, who knows what was there before the barracks were built in Fascist times, under Mussolini. This was where the young Italians did their boot training when military service was still obligatory. Up until 2004 every young man had to do a year as a soldier (unless he was going to college in which case he could be deferred). Now the barracks are mostly empty and the city is still trying to figure out what to do with them. They housed 5000 soldiers. When I first came to Orvieto in 1958, this area was quite different, with soldiers wandering the streets after hours until curfew. They far outnumbered the tourists. The recruits came from all over Italy, and there were some who didn't even know how to read or write. For many, their year of military service was a year lost. But for others it opened new horizons. Think of Gavino Ledda, son of a Sardinian shepherd, for whom enlisting in the army gave him a chance to get away from the poverty and brutality of the backward environment in which he was trapped on the island. His determination eventually took him to the university, where he became a scholar of the Italian language. His autobiographic novel, *Padre Padrone*, was also made into a movie.

We pass the Carabinieri headquarters and the prison building across the way. It's supposed to be quite a nice prison, as prisons go. Years ago I was once summoned to translate in an interrogation, forget now what the young man had done. I was however very impressed by the judge, tall, handsome, wearing a Zorro cloak, who said all he was interested in was the truth, for the story was rather full of contradictions.

Then comes a small car-filled piazza on our right overlooked by the church of San Domenico. We can only visualize what it must have looked like back in the twelfth century when it was on the outskirts of the town itself, abandoned and with a dubious reputation. Originally there was nothing here but a small parish church, possibly built on the site of a temple to Minerva. Certainly replacing it with a large church and convent would in a sense redeem the site. The patron saint, Dominic, is known for his attempts to convert the Cathars in southern France, and as founder of the Order of Preachers, or the Dominican Order. It was one of the first Dominican churches to be built (1233-39).

The church as it is now with its modest entrance makes one wonder what happened to make it look as if someone had been playing around and trying to fit various architectural elements together. There seems to be no rhyme or reason to the way in which the alternating basalt and travertine courses, in that striped pattern we'll see in the cathedral, hem tufa walls that look as if they had been broken off and were not going anywhere. The façade too is particularly anonymous. You may wonder why I am taking you to what some would consider a minor church before taking you to the Cathedral, but there's a story here that brings San Domenico close to my own family history. While the church was transformed more than once, for an explanation of its current state we have to return to Fascist times when the church was to be torn down to make way for a women's physical education academy. Actually the academy still exists over to the left of the church, with the convent courtyard, only now it is used by the Finance Police to train their officers. As luck would have it, my father-in-law was superintendent of Fine Arts in Perugia in those years and therefore in charge of protecting the works of art and architecture in Orvieto, which belonged to the province of Perugia. His family was from Orvieto, and his father's tomb is in the cemetery here. Although he was supposedly to do away with San Domenico, one of the first dedicated to that saint, he was determined to save at least the aisle with Arnolfo di Cambio's tomb monument to Cardinal de Braye, dating to around 1282. Renato Ricci, the Fascist party official, head of the youth movement, wanted the whole church pulled down, no matter what." *I'll surround the church with my cohorts*", he thundered. To which my father-in-law answered, "*In that case I'll call in my "carabinieri".* The minister of popular culture succeeded in getting Ricci to back down and so we still have at least the transept of the church of San Domenico.

I guess we have Arnolfo di Cambio and my father-in-law to thank for saving the church, even if only in part. On our left, upon entering, is the tomb of Cardinal de Braye by Arnolfo, one of the most important sculptors and architects of the late 13th century. It was this monument that Arnolfo Bizzarri was so adamant about saving. The French cardinal, who died in 1282, is shown wearing his cardinal regalia (note the gloves) as two choirboys draw aside the curtains to reveal him lying on his catafalque. But since Arnolfo is standing over there looking quizzically up at the figure of the Virgin Mary in the gable maybe we can even ask him about it.

"I'm not so sure you've got all these elements put together as I had planned. I hear the tomb has been dismantled and moved more than once. I hope you don't feel that I sort of hoodwinked you in the figure of Mary for I didn't carve her from scratch. It was too tempting to use this ancient Roman statue and transform her by adding the Child. Might she not have been Juno, queen of the gods who kept special watch over all aspects of women's lives? After all churches dedicated to the Virgin Mary were often built on the sites of Roman temples to the virgin goddess Diana. If you could see the back part of this monument, you would notice that it was unfinished. Again I did that on purpose, for I always left the unseen parts unworked. St Mark up there on the left is presenting the kneeling cardinal to the Madonna, for death is a passage to eternity, while St. Dominic on the right is interceding with her for the cardinal. I hope you also appreciate all those mosaic inserts that lend light to the background with their glitter. I particularly like this technique that is known as Cosmatesque, after the Roman family who popularized it using fragments of ancient columns for the colored stones. The overall effect of my monument was quite different with parts of the statues also gilded and colored."

The panels on either side of the entrance explain the history of the church in detail, but they are, alas, only in Italian. Perhaps I can eventually get around to translating them. In the chapel to the right of the apse, the wooden figure of the crucified Christ is said to have told Thomas of Aquinas that he had written well of Him when he was preparing the office for the miracle of Transubstantiation. I find it curious that the crucifix with its stress on suffering is definitely not Italian, but northern, perhaps Flemish, probably twelfth-thirteenth century. Makes me wonder where it came from. The importance of Orvieto comes to the fore when we realize that Thomas was teaching theology here in 1261-65. It helps to remember that saints and popes were after all only persons, although sometimes they themselves seem to have thought otherwise. Certainly one can't always approve of what they did and how they acted, but we can try and understand them to a certain extent. Thomas, for instance, seems to have been super intellectual and I found a student's prayer by him that I rather like. It says "*Grant me a penetrating mind to understand, a retentive memory, method and ease in learning, the lucidity to comprehend, and abundant grace in expressing myself.*" Now if I can follow these precepts, certainly what I am doing here makes more sense.

St. Thomas, a true teacher, is quite willing to answer some of our questions. "*You may have wondered what that shield with a dog holding a torch in its jaws is doing on the choir loft over the altar. Dominic's mother ardently had wanted a child, and as recounted in Jacopo da Varagine's Golden Legend, she had a dream where a dog holding a torch appeared, a sign that the child she was to bear would set the world on fire with his preaching. So we are Dominicans, named after Saint Dominic, and the dog is a reference to Domini canus, "dog of the Lord". If you've been in Florence, the best example is the fresco in what is known as the Spanish Chapel in Santa Maria Novella, where black and white hounds stand for the Dominican friars. There's a lot to be learned from Jacopo da Varagine and his collection of the lives of the saints. I'm told it was a best seller throughout Europe.* "

Wonder what Arnolfo di Cambio thinks about the Petrucci chapel underneath the apse (remember that what is now the nave was once the transept, that part of the church that crosses at right angles to the nave before the apse or choir) after the rest had been torn down. I'm sure he approved of the mosaic floor, for after all he did use mosaic inlays a lot, as in his monument to the cardinal by the entrance. The underground chapel dates to between 1516 and 1522 and was built for the exiled Sienese family of the Petrucci by Sanmicheli, an artist/architect/sculptor from Verona. Located under what is now the apse, there is a staircase leading down on the left and another that brings you back up on the right of the altar. It could be a sort of *Anastasis*, or resurrection after death. The chapel itself is in the shape of an octagon inscribed in a square. Baptisteries were commonly octagonal in plan, symbolizing a new beginning, the first day of resurrection. Perhaps another reference to a new life, as in baptism.

It is a calming experience to sit in the chapel, with its mosaic floor, and let the geometric harmony and the contrasting colors of the white walls, the grey basalt and red brick sink in. Curiously enough, up on top, in the floor of the apse, are bas-relief sculptures with an opening at the center that looks down on the tomb. As is so often the case with Renaissance chapels, inspiration was drawn from the Holy Sepulcher in Jerusalem, where death is followed by resurrection or rebirth.

And the portal of the church? That was purloined from the church of Santo Spirito degli Armeni on the Tamburino, that old Etruscan/Romanesque route that led to Rome via Bolsena. The church there had had to be abandoned when the road that led to Orvieto, and along which it was built, changed course.

American Study abroad programs, Via Pecorelli – a cardinal's apartment

Continuing on we'll pass first what is now the specialization center for the Italian Finanza, which encloses the cloister of San Domenico, and then the former court building, where the American university study abroad programs have their headquarters. Orvieto has become a center for American college and university study abroad programs. Gordon College has its headquarters in the Servite convent, the University of Arizona has full semester programs, and then there is St. Anselm from Manchester NH, and Kansas, and Illinois, Drew University. The students generally fall in love with Orvieto and are happy to get back "home" after a frenetic day in Rome.

A small street that goes downhill ends up in a car park with another entrance to the ring road. Fifty years ago these were fields and my children would play here and bring home pieces of medieval pottery they had discovered. The house on the left as we start uphill on Via Pecorelli is where Mario and I lived when we first came to Orvieto. Those two narrow Gothic windows were once the private chapel of the cardinal owner, before becoming our bedroom. Cardinal Cerretti (born to a farming family in Bardano, just a few kilometers from Orvieto) held the title of apostolic delegate to Australia, among others. There's a painting of him in the town hall, dating to 1930. He is resting one hand on a large book but from what his biographer has to say, it seems unlikely that it was of great interest to him. A huge Webster's, with gilt tipped pages, which had belonged to him, came with the apartment. I wonder now whether he had ever opened that dictionary, since he was described as never having been seen reading a book.

Our apartment occupied half of what is known as the *piano nobile*, the first floor, while the services or "help" were housed in the attic or on the ground floor. In Via Pecorelli there was a silent butler in the premises by the entrance, which once brought food up to the cardinal's dining room. Our kitchen ceiling had frescoes of landscapes and we had a kerosene stove for heating. Our landlady, who was certainly in her eighties, was the cardinal's sister. When I had to leave for work in Rome, several times a week, if I came back late, at four o'clock my daytime help, Aurora, would leave Claudio with Antinisca, my landlady's housekeeper. I was amazed one morning when I found (what was her name? oh yes, Yolanda) in the courtyard behind the house pouring boiling water over laundry covered with ashes. *"That's how you bleach sheets"*, she explained. I had learned something new.

Across from our apartment was a grade school, in a building that was once a home for impoverished spinsters. Further up was an oven overseen by Bruno, a small man who must have had muscular dystrophy since he always had to support himself on the wall as he moved, and Antonietta, his live-wire wife. This was where bread was baked and at Easter the women would bring their Easter breads, flavored with cinnamon and rosolio, or with bits of cheese, to Bruno. My sister-in-law used to get up at all hours of the night to check if the breads, wrapped in a quilt to keep them warm, were rising properly. Bruno also roasted the porchetta – the fire had blazed for hours so that the bricks could absorb the heat. When the time came, the ashes were raked aside to make way for the whole pig stuffed with garlic and wild fennel. Eight hours later it would be a golden color, with a crisp crackling crust. I used to love it Sundays when I would take my chicken smothered in potatoes and rosemary to the oven. Bruno would always add some of the fat from the roasting pig, giving that chicken a flavor impossible to capture nowadays.

In the piazza off to the left is the Trattoria del Orso. That truly has changed. When I first came and needed some wine, all I had to do was take a bottle up to the trattoria. I used to feel a bit self-conscious as the only woman there among the groups of old men playing cards and with a quartino, or quarter of a liter, of wine by their side. I would hand my bottle to the owner, who would fill it from a wine cask at the back. The Orso, or Bear, is still a trattoria, but now the customers are tourists in the know and the interiors are by the Michelangeli.

Curiously enough the alimentari or grocer's on Piazza della Repubblica is still there. Casa del Parmigiano. It hasn't even changed its name. I don't remember who the shopkeepers were in 1958 when I would buy, say, a quarter pound of rice or sugar, weighed out in a brown paper cone. And trying to figure out what baking powder was! Turned out it was known as Royal. And coffee? Best place was a shop known as I Svizzeri, the Swiss, since the owner originally came from Switzerland. Great thing was that they roasted their coffee beans and some mornings the whole street was permeated by the fragrance of roasting coffee. Of course you had to know how you wanted it ground. This was also the place where you got the liqueurs, one of which was a cinnamon flavored rosolio, as well as the leavening agent, for your Easter "cake" or Christmas cookies. And you bought things by the gram.

Next door to the Orso there's a goldsmith with the intriguing name of Trequattrini or Three pennies. Give him a stone or gem you have kept in a drawer for years and want finally to make the most of. He will design a striking one-of-a-kind brooch or pendant for you.

Cavour, Italy before being Italy, Palazzo dei Sette, Palazzo del Popolo

Or one can continue up Via Pecorelli and end up in Piazza della Repubblica, to turn left up Corso Cavour. Again, unless you've boned up on Italian history you probably don't remember that Cavour was a leading figure in the nineteenth-century movement for Italian unification, the Risorgimento. Throughout history, the story of what we now call Italy was that of small city-states, like Florence, Milan, Perugia, etc. And Orvieto too. They were always fighting each other for power, and territory. You know, even now there are echoes of this in the Italian identity. A person will first of all tell you whatever town or even quarter he was born in, say Monterubiaglio, then admit that it is part of the district of Orvieto, which belongs to the province of Terni (although on the whole I think most Orvietani would rather belong to Perugia), then the region of Umbria and finally, maybe they will get around to saying they are Italian.

While there are palazzi along the way by important architects, unless you're an architecture buff, let's just continue to the crossing with Via Duomo, with Palazzo dei Sette, or dei Signori Sette, and the Torre del Moro, on our left. If you feel up to it, you can climb to the top of the tower, home to two bells, one of which bears the twenty-five symbols of the professions. You risk being deafened if you're there at noon when the bells toll as you are looking out over the rooftops of Orvieto. From here you can see just how the town is divided into quarters and what the four poles are. The religious center is of course the Cathedral, the Palazzo del Capitano is the military center, the Palazzo dei Signori Sette, with the heads of the guilds, I would call Wall Street, and then Piazza della Repubblica is the political center with the town hall.

The large building on the square behind the Palazzo dei Sette is Palazzo del Capitano del Popolo. Begun in the late thirteenth century, the bell tower was added in 1315. The upper floor was the residence of the Capitano del Popolo, Podestà and Signori Sette. In 1463 the Monte di Pietà, or institutional pawnbroker, was established in the lower part, while in 1651 the Monte Frumentario was a sort of insurance for the farmers, providing a supply of seeds for the coming year. Up to then it had housed a *Studium*, for law and theology, the equivalent of a university. In the sixteenth century there was also a theater in the upper part, sponsored in 1680 by Queen Christine of Sweden when she visited Orvieto.

Talking about theater, this was where I saw my first movie in Italy when I visited Orvieto in 1955. It was a western and might have had Gary Cooper; it was over 60 years ago so I don't really remember, except that of course that whoever it was, Gary Cooper or John Wayne, spoke perfect Italian. Films are always dubbed in Italy and I must say they do an excellent job. Still it is sometimes odd when a voice you identify with a certain actor, has a completely different tonality.

The palazzo was skillfully restored in 1984-9 to become a convention center, respecting the original architecture. If some kind of event is in progress, you can probably wander in. Note how the modern stairs don't impinge on the medieval masonry, and how the huge tufa blocks with Etruscan letters on them down below, possibly part of an Etruscan temple, act as backdrop to one of the smaller auditoriums. Medieval remains, including part of a reservoir and of an aqueduct, are visible in the corridor. On the upper floor, only the ghosts of the rich fresco decoration with the coats of arms of the various occupants of the palazzo still cling to the walls. This is the Sala dei Quattrocento, which does seat 400 people, even though the name is modern. In the fourteenth century the Orvietani would meet down below to settle important questions and administer justice. Technically the equipment for the new use of this "container" is extremely modern with translators' booths and headsets, projectors and microphones, and whatever else is needed for conferences and meetings. It is extremely well heated so that in attending a lecture in winter, one has to shed at least two layers.

Right across from the Palazzo del Popolo is one of the most fascinating hotels in Orvieto – the Hotel Reale. It's full of history and when you go in you seem to be going back in time at least a century. A tiny elevator takes you up to the reception hall – your luggage had been taken over by an attendant down below, and by the time you exit from the elevator, your bags are already there. Someone once said it would be perfect for the Addams family. A little old man in uniform, who looks as if he were a hundred, takes your documents at a desk where the original checking-in apparatus still takes up most of the space. A hundred years ago or more? Your room has high frescoed ceilings and a bath with a yellow marble tub. So and so, some royalty, stayed here you are told, while you wonder how you will get in after dark.

Piazza del Popolo is also where the market is held on Thursday and Saturday. One still gets farmers from the surrounding countryside coming in. If you're buying a melon, Paolo, the vendor from Bolsena, will ask you when you intend to eat it, to make sure he gives you the one that will be ripe tomorrow or the day after. There are now also benches with a medley of clothing marked 5 or 10 euro. Great if you have the patience to riffle through this jumble, and if they have your size. Flowers, plants, kitchenware, hardware, shoes, linens – eggs from free-range chickens wrapped in twos in newspaper, and of course the seasonal produce. Artichokes from November through April, strawberries generally around Corpus Domini, agretti or friar's beard that looks like grass, persimmons only in fall. Christmas is cardoons. Gone are the days when little old ladies brought in live rabbits or chickens and kerchiefs of wild herbs gathered in the fields.

Market in years past - Photo by Erika Bizzarri

You may also have asked yourself whose bust that is at the bottom of the flight of stairs leading up to the Sala dei Quattrocento. For festivals when the Orvietani wear their marvelous medieval costumes, they process down these stairs and it's a great place as backdrop for photographs. Back to the gentleman whose bust keeps an eye on the piazza. He's Adolfo Cozza, previously mentioned, a sculptor and archaeologist, who designed the funicular that takes visitors from the railroad station to Orvieto.

Mancinelli Theater, the Corso, Servite church

Over on the Corso, that building with a portico is the Mancinelli Theater, built thanks to a theater consortium of citizens who then presented it to the city of Orvieto in 1866. Its one hundred and fifty years certainly doesn't make it old by Italian standards. When one thinks of theater, generally one thinks of plays, of musicals on Broadway. If we want to go back to the history of theater, aside from the ancient Greeks, the beginnings in Orvieto would have been the miracle plays, meant to elucidate the unlettered and put the fear of God in them with representations of the fires of hell, or amaze them with the miracles of the lives of the saints. In the 16th century, Orvieto did already have a theater in the Palazzo del Popolo. In the beginning, theater meant opera, what they call *opera lirica* in Italian. So it is only fitting that this theater is named after one of its native sons, Luigi Mancinelli, a famous conductor and composer who conducted at the Met in New York and in Covent Gardens in London for 20 years.

I love to think of what theater used to be like – going back to Shakespeare when the dandies sat around the perimeter of the stage to be seen, rather than to see. Theater used to be for the elite, particularly when it evolved into boxes and the orchestra. Boxes were the center of life in the theater with people exchanging visits, eating and drinking, playing cards and some of them had curtains which could be drawn for privacy and who knows what went on behind them. The orchestra was for the bourgeois, shopkeepers, students. My first visit to the theater years ago was for a Verdi opera and everyone in Orvieto, including the mechanic and the plumber, were there. I am reminded of attending a baseball game in Atlanta, which seems to me also included eating and drinking and exchanging visits.

So obviously, one must go inside. If not for a performance, sometimes opera, then in the theater season for either dramas or comedies (I find it strange that the Italians call them all "comedie", whether they make you laugh or are tear-jerkers, since they all originated in the sixteenth-century Comedia dell'Arte. Although of course, there is also Dante's *Divine Comedy*, which has nothing laughable in it), or perhaps a jazz concert, or simply for a tour. The interior is a beautiful example of nineteenth-century theater art with ceiling paintings of allegorical figures. There are representations of the hours, floating among the clouds, the Muses and the four seasons, as well as classic composers and poets. But go into what the Italians call the foyer, which is strangely enough upstairs, into the realm of the four seasons, poetry and harmony, and painted statues in niches. This is one of the places where you can have a civil wedding – and which is where my archaeologist son was married, by the mayor, with violins playing up in the balcony. The other sites for civil weddings are the town hall, and of all things, the caves of Orvieto Underground. Lighting for the theater was originally provided by a hydroelectric power plant in the woods near Sugano. Again, quite a novelty for the times.

Most striking however, and again we are getting a lesson in history, is the stage curtain depicting the Goths driven from the city of Orvieto by Belisarius, the Byzantine emperor Justinian's general. This happened in the sixth century when Belisarius laid siege to the city and starved the Goths into surrender. Sound familiar? Eight centuries earlier the Romans had laid siege to the Etruscans and forced them to surrender. Can you imagine any other way of conquering a city with such indomitable defenses?

Hopefully you'll be here for a performance. If it's between Christmas and New Year's, you have a chance to hear the best in jazz with "Umbria Jazz Winter". Plays or concerts generally don't start till 9:30 so that it will be after midnight when you leave.

If it was a play, the theater will just have disgorged its mostly middle-aged crowd. Together we slowly filter down into the street, some of us swallowed up by the side street next to the theater on our way to the car, or we might just linger and move up the Corso past the cafes where young people, home for the weekend from university and bringing their laundry for their mothers to wash and iron, are chatting outside, holding a glass of wine, enveloped in a cloud of music so loud one wonders how they can hear each other.

Corso Cavour, generally called just plain Corso, is, together with Via Duomo, the main drag and is lined with shops and restaurants. The post office is next to the theater, as well as a palazzo by Sanmicheli, the architect who designed the chapel in San Domenico. It's at number 149-51. It has a rightness of proportions that makes it recognizable, particularly after you've seen the Petrucci Chapel. As you move down towards the theater, past various restaurants and shops, there's one with strange paintings by someone named Verdirosi. They all seem to be of an emaciated old man with a skinny dog, both sadly wending their way through an arid landscape. The paintings are all the same and I wonder about the painter, for never have I seen anything more joyless. A bit further down is a ceramics shop called L'Arpia, perhaps one of the only places in Orvieto where real traditional Orvieto ceramics are still made.

Way down, just before Piazza Cahen, is the Servite church. You may not think it's up to the other churches you've been looking at but I've been curious about it ever since I came to Orvieto. For years I had been looking for the painting all the guidebooks say is by Coppo di Marcovaldo and that it was in this church. I subsequently learned the painting was in restoration and had to wait till 1984 to see it. And to think I came to Orvieto in 1958! It's now in the museum of the Opera del Duomo.

Via del Duomo, heart of Orvieto, Palazzo Netti, San Giuseppe, L'Orvietan

It's probably about time to take a good look at the Cathedral. I suppose that's one of the reasons why you came to Orvieto.

There are a few things to note as we walk up Via del Duomo. Besides the souvenir shops that is. Not many have real Orvieto ceramics, and I'll bet much of it was made in China. The typical Orvieto ceramics in their traditional medieval style are simple dark brown and turquoise or green designs, often with the head of a man or woman, a queen, a mermaid. L'Arpia, a shop on the Corso, near Piazza Cahen, still makes traditional medieval style pottery.

A few steps up Via del Duomo there's a small square with a couple of benches. It is here that you are sure to find the same old-timers exchanging views on politics every morning. Or you might find them a bit further up, at the Bar Duomo to which they migrate after an initial stop at Montanucci's.

Turn around and observe the palazzo bordering the square with a passageway that takes you back to the Corso. It is the portal though that strikes the attentive observer. How curious that it is squeezed in between the windows on either side. You'd think the architect would have left a breathing space between the doorway and the window surrounds.

So let's eavesdrop on those two figures hovering in the background, who have just finished a game of cards. We're already in the late nineteenth century, although the portal dates to 1583 and is by Ippolito Scalza, the Orvieto architect whose hand can be identified almost everywhere, including the Cathedral where he was capo maestro. That doorway with its anthropomorphic elements was, believe it or not, once on a palazzo in the street that leads out of Piazza Duomo, to the right of Palazzo Soliano. Palazzo Buzi, now Mercedari. Can't you just hear Aldobrandi Netti, the owner of this palazzo that goes by the name of Gualterio, gloating as he slams down the winning card?

"Sorry, but your portal now is mine!" Now what I've just told you may be a legend, but it's too good not to include here.

The little church of San Giuseppe on the small piazza is dedicated to St. Joseph, patron saint of Orvieto since 1652. Even a left-wing (communist) government respects this working-class saint. On March 19th, the saint's feast day and also by the way Father's Day in Italy, there are celebrations in his honor with the band playing in the square, and offerings of the *fritelle* di San Giuseppe, sweet rice fritters as well as small cream puffs with pink ricotta custard, made only then. That's what I like about Orvieto – you can't get special foods like this at any other time. There are a few other festivity-linked foods, like *panettone* at Christmas, but I'll tell you about them later.

Via del Duomo somehow is the heart of Orvieto. There's a specialty shop for local produce called I Fratelli, the Brothers, with a boar's head outside. The owner, Emilio, has the elegant grace of a dancer as he cuts you a hundred grams of prosciutto or advises you as to which pecorino cheese or boar sausages are best. He can also vacuum pack your purchases. Across the way is another jeweler's, inspired by Etruscan granulation work or Roman coins. The shop next to them displays a multitude of multicolored scarves and bags from the Orient. That's what I would have had in my shop fifty years ago, when there weren't any others like them in Orvieto.

Summer in Orvieto also means street musicians. Most of them are what one could call amateurs – playing just as an excuse to make a bit of money. There's a thin bookish looking young woman with a harp. There are some with a sax or perhaps making believe with a recording of jazz. Or some who combine showmanship with music of a sorts – jiggling and dancing till you wonder they don't get out of joint. And then there was Peter.

I was walking up Via del Duomo, had just passed San Giuseppe, when I heard some Bach floating up the street. A cello. And quite good. I turned back to see who was responsible and found a slender lean man, a baseball cap pulled down backwards, surrounded by a few tourists. But what stopped me short as I listened were his sandaled feet. They were absolutely clean! As if he had just washed them before beginning his day. I asked him what he was playing and it turned out he was American. He taught and played in New York and came to Italy every summer, wandering from one north Italian town to another (he didn't trust southern Italy), and evidently made a goodly sum. Every morning, before playing he would run for an hour or so. Orvieto was his last stop before returning to the airport and home. And as such, it turned into a tradition. His last night we would meet for dinner, although he always wanted to see the sunset first. He would tell me about his adventures, perhaps play a bit in the evening, and then I would wait for the next year to come around. That was Peter. A free soul.

Next stop might be Vicolo degli Artigiani, a side street on your right filled with craft shops. Indeed one, called the Wizard of Oz, is unique, and seems to stock just about everything from a life-size Betty Boop statue (nothing to do with Orvieto) to globes with snow falling on the Cathedral, to reproductions of posters with movie stars of the 30s and 40s. The other shops have more local products, such as hand-woven textiles, ceramics, and olivewood bowls as well as pecorino cheese. There's also an artist's studio (Michele Golia), where Paolo Golia's black pottery, a rediscovery of the secret for making that typically Etruscan black bucchero, is featured.

Back on Via Duomo, just before getting to the Restaurant Maurizio, opened over a hundred years ago, is a shop called L'Orvietan. There's a story here, too, of course. The owner, Lamberto, is a real entrepreneur.

"I've copyrighted the name of my shop, and what it originally referred to. L'Orvietan. Would you like to sample this after-dinner liqueur? It's quite strong and will help your digestion. I had to do a lot of research before I could, let's say, resuscitate it. L'Orvietan. Goes back to the beginning of the seventeenth century, sold as a cure-all, a miraculous potion, and was officially approved by the Sun King in France. The original vender hailed from Orvieto, hence the name, and I rather think he was a charlatan. This potion was, however, so famous that even Walter Scott mentioned it in his novels. What are the ingredients? Ah, that remains a

secret. Don't want others making this although I can tell you that it has all of 25 herbs in it."

While it hasn't been approved by the sun king, I have my own version of an aperitif. Or I should say my son's for he always insists I make some each year and we now have bottles going back to 2012. So just what is this liqueur, almost black as pitch? There is of course a story here too. St. John the Baptist. His feast day is June 24th and the little town of San Lorenzo Nuovo celebrates it with a market particularly for local products (used to be animals) which has now taken over every little street. We always go with friends to get our yearly supply of garlic braided into ropes. But also to celebrate St. John by sitting at a long table in one of the cellars that then leads back into a cave. One buys a bottle of Cannaiola, that local fragrant red wine that goes surprisingly well with fried lake fish, porchetta, pecorino cheese, and for the braver souls, pickled eel. What has this to do with nocino? That's when you're supposed to pick the walnuts, still not with a hard shell. Some sources say only virgins can pick them, and they have to be barefooted. Then you quarter 33 of the nuts and let them sit for 40 days in a bath of pure alcohol in the sun. After this you filter, and add some syrup. Then there is still another wait, for the bottled nocino must age for at least six months.

I also love the tradition of acqua odorosa, perfumed water. The day before you pick all the fragrant plants you can think of, like roses and lavender, sage and rosemary, scotch broom, but above all what they call erba della Madonna, Mary's herb. Floating in a large bowl all night, by the light of the moon, the morning of St.John's day you wash your face in this fantastically fragrant water. It all has to do with the summer solstice.

Clock Tower, plague, cathedral workyard, Marino Moretti, Livio Orazio Valentini

That clock tower on the other side of the street is known as the tower of Maurizio, after the automaton on top who strikes the hours. Maurizio is however probably simply a misinterpretation of the word *muriccio*, or construction site. One wouldn't have expected it to be built in 1348, for that was when the plague appeared in Orvieto. The Black Death was mowing down the populations of most of Europe, with 70% of the inhabitants of Siena and Florence succumbing. Orvieto seems to have gotten away with 50%. Descriptions are really apocalyptic. Carts going through the streets to collect the dead, children, mothers, whole families. This was when the young people in Boccaccio's *Decameron* took refuge in the countryside and told stories to wile away the time. The economy couldn't come to a standstill, and this, one of Italy's oldest mechanical clocks, was built in Orvieto. There's a webcam that lets you see the clockwork mechanism on a screen in a small room in the tower entrance, just before Marino Moretti's ceramic shop. Can you imagine what it must have meant at the time? Workers no longer had to be "clocked" by hand-rung bells. The notary who kept track of their hours now had a precise way of annotating when they came in and when they stopped work. The cathedral archives in Orvieto are amazing for they give us a day-by-day rundown of what was involved in the construction of the Cathedral. We know what materials arrived and what they cost. We know what the workers' hours were and that in summer the 14-hour day had three breaks – half-hour in the morning and afternoon and an hour for lunch. In winter they only had a half hour's break in the morning and an hour for lunch for a total of a ten-hour working day. The bell-ringer not only strikes the bell but is actually dialoging with the bell, to which an inscription on his belt and on the bell bears witness. "*Between you and me, bell, let's make a pact: you are here to cry out and I am here to act.*" To which the bell responds: "*Fine, but take it easy for if you hit me too hard, I'll break and then what do we do?*"

Perhaps your eye has been caught by the brilliantly glazed vases, large and small, and the witty tiles, in the shop next door. Marino Moretti's ceramics are in a class by themselves. He is not simply a potter – he is an artist, and an example of the part a family sometimes plays in the future of one of its members. Marino's grandfather and his father both had fantastic collections of medieval pottery, and as a teen-ager he was already experimenting with glazes. One of my prized possessions now is a deep blue globular vase with a turquoise interior. It sits next to my computer with an aura all its own, and seems to be whispering quietly, hoping I will catch the words. Marino gradually developed his own artistic vocabulary, and now has a studio in a castle in the little town of Viceno. He's always happy to have visitors, and you can watch him make perfect circles on a dish or incise a design using a porcupine quill. A porcupine quill, you say? Yes, but from an Old World crested porcupine, a much larger creature with a magnificent crest of quills, not your smaller New World porcupine that hails from a different family. Sometimes you may even catch sight of one or of a whole family in the headlights of your car as you move along a country road. Porcupine quills are also ideal for holding the tufts of Marino's brushes. While most of Marino's pottery is made of the local red clay, in the last few years he has added porcelain to his repertory.

I suppose I could go into a history of porcelain here but if you're interested, a particularly good read is *The White Road* by Edward De Waal, a ceramist himself. If the public library is open, go see Marino's benches in the garden or children's playground, with the four seasons depicted in glorious glowing colors. The source of his imagery is medieval, but it is his own fantasy that makes them unique.

Walking up Via Maitani to the public library, we also go back in time. This was where Marino and Livio Orazio Valentini once both had their studios. It is probably late afternoon since Valentini was not an early riser. The teen-age ceramic artist is rather in awe of this mature artist as they compare notes on the pretty women passing by, and bathe in the reflected light of the magnificent façade glowing in the afternoon sun. Most of the tourists, who often lie in the middle of the street trying to get it all in on their cameras, have left. The piazza belongs to Valentini and Marino as the painter comes up with philosophical remarks on color and how the Orvietani are too tied to the past and have no idea what he is doing.

"See those swallows Marino? Love to watch them swoop around the pinnacles. Never did figure out how they never collide. They are free. But our spirits have been chained, constrained, by man. God? Well, He meant for our spirits too to fly free. Then along come the Nazis and send people like me to Buchenwald. Oh, look. There still are a couple of tourists in the piazza. Did you see those two young things that just went by? Seems to me skirts are getting skimpier and skimpier. Or that woman – must have been German or maybe American – sure wasn't Italian. She was big, really big, and was wearing a sort of white kaftan with huge colored circles on it – real bull's eyes. Can you imagine anything more striking? Like enormous bull's eyes. Guess we'd better get back to work. The sun has really set fire to the mosaics."

In continuing along Via Maitani we pass the Hotel Maitani, now closed, with its triton column. Next door there's a palazzo with a facade covered with monochrome sgraffito decorations depicting the fundamental virtues and elements (I think it's 19th century). Not many raise their eyes to look at it. It once belonged to Netti, the man who first gave electricity to the city. Now the palazzo belongs to a former waiter who somehow succeeded in climbing the social financial ladder and even bought MGM, (but didn't keep it for long). Rumor has it that he had private jets, owned hotels, dined with Kissinger, etc. With reference to MGM, he supposedly said that it was like a woman: ... the important thing was to conquer her, then whatever happens, happens..." He invented his own coat of arms, to be seen next to the entrance, and has been considered the quintessential adventurer. A film of his life has even been made – The Lion from Orvieto. He does sound as if he belonged in the period of the Medicis. They were not originally nobles either but certainly made a name for themselves. I've never met him but wonder if he wasn't the waiter Coates mentioned in his book on Italian Hill Towns, who, as they were dining in Piazza del Duomo, whisked away an unfinished omelet when his friend lifted his fork to make a remark.

Since we were on our way to the library, let's make sure it's open for it has a rather irregular schedule. This is due mostly to a lack of personnel, one of the problems that afflict so much of Italy. Basically, however, it is a lack of funding, for were there enough money, the personnel could be trained. The library itself, where I volunteered for a while, is truly avant-garde, even if it is in a thirteenth-century building. Books, including some in English, as well as DVDs, can be borrowed; all you need is a library card, free. If you're interested in listening and watching recordings of any kind, there is also what they call the Sala Eufonica, a top-notch multimedia audio-video auditorium. I believe there's only one other like it in Italy. When they moved the books from the library's former site in one of the high school buildings several blocks away, students helped by forming a human chain to pass the boxes from one to another. Once more there are layers of history here in this building – a former convent, military garrison, school, and now a library with manuscripts on parchment and *incunabula*, books printed before 1501, vintage photographs, as well as the latest books and journals.

Back to Via Maitani, closed to traffic, with that fantastic façade at the end (or is it the beginning?) drawing us, like a magnet, back to Piazza Duomo. Let's move over to the end of the square on the side where Marino's shop is, stopping for an ice cream cone. The owner used to be Patrizia Pasqualetti, who sold all rights and is now, of all places, in San Francisco. Her ice cream shop was chosen to participate in the Italian month at the UN in New York. When I had my shop I used to take a quick run over afternoons for a chocolate and mint cone. In case you need a rest room, there are steps leading down out of the piazza to the public loo, although often it's simpler to go to a cafe and order a glass of water or coffee and use theirs.

The next stop, down those steps, is the Hotel Duomo; you might want to stay there next time you're in Orvieto. But what interests us right now are the paintings by Livio Orazio Valentini in the reception hall. Valentini very much belonged to the twentieth century, experiencing the horrors of war and imprisonment. Yet his later work is all about color – about the joy of living. It is often the case that an artist is not truly acknowledged in his native country and Valentini never got his full due until he became artist-in-residence at the University of South

Carolina Aiken, subsequently painting an important mural for one of the university buildings.

The work of an artist, Valentini and Signorelli included, tells us as much about the times in which the artist lived as about himself. If you've already been in the Cathedral, you'll be struck by the fact that some of Livio's paintings here in the Hotel Duomo are studies of the Signorelli frescoes in the Cathedral. People are particularly taken by the man with green buttocks whom Livio has isolated, somehow identifying with the violence of the figure. There's an incredible tension here, as if the solid matter were straining to escape its bounds.

If you need an explanation of why Livio "copied" Signorelli, let's let him speak for himself:

"Signorelli's frescoes reflect the chaotic times he lived in. The end of the world? Perhaps today there are even more signs that the end is approaching than there were in Signorelli's time. What better way to understand what he was trying to do, to express, than by analyzing his figures. Reinterpreting another artist's work is one way of doing this. We can't get away from our own time though and that's one of the reasons it is so difficult to successfully forge an earlier work."

The Duomo, Maitani, Cathars

Back up to Piazza Duomo. Might be time to take a closer look at the Cathedral. Do try to be here when the sun is setting and the mosaics on the façade glow gold. True, not everyone has always been enthusiastic about the façade. One traveler described the cathedral as a peacock in a hencoop. Still there's nothing quite like it. Not all, but the greater part, of the Grand Tour visitors agreed. Mostly from England, they came in groups, one might call them cultural pilgrims, for in the seventeenth through nineteenth centuries anyone worth his while had to take a trip to Italy to see, in their words, "the true cradle of civilization." Traveling certainly wasn't easy those days, going over the Alps along narrow trails with steep chasms falling down sheer on either side. On the whole the travelers were attracted by the Roman past of Italy, rather than the Gothic or Medieval periods or even the Renaissance. They often came along the coast on their way to Rome but some did take the route that passed through Orvieto. Travel in those days was not for the faint-hearted. You had to be willing to suffer bedbugs and poor food.

Maybe an exception was Charles Dickens, as we learn in his *Pictures from Italy*, written in 1846. He was quite contented with what was served at the osteria he stopped at near Siena. Note particularly his reference to Orvieto wine!

"We had the usual dinner in this solitary house; and a very good dinner it is, when you are used to it. There is something with a vegetable or some rice in it which is a sort of shorthand or arbitrary character for soup, and which tastes very well, when you have flavoured it with plenty of grated cheese, lots of salt, and abundance of pepper. There is the half fowl of which this soup has been made. There is a stewed pigeon, with the gizzards and livers of himself and other birds stuck all round him. There is a bit of roast beef, the size of a small French roll. There are a scrap of Parmesan cheese, and five little withered apples, all huddled together on a small plate, and crowding one upon the other, as if each were trying to save itself from the chance of being eaten. Then there is coffee; and then there is bed. You don't mind brick floors; you

don't mind yawning doors, nor banging windows; you don't mind your own horses being stabled under the bed: and so close, that every time a horse coughs or sneezes, he wakes you. If you are good-humoured to the people about you, and speak pleasantly, and look cheerful, take my word for it you may be well entertained in the very worst Italian Inn, and always in the most obliging manner, and may go from one end of the country to the other (despite all stories to the contrary) without any great trial of your patience anywhere. Especially, when you get such wine in flasks, as the Orvieto, and the Monte Pulciano." (Pictures from Italy, 1846)

One of the most famous travelers was Joseph William Turner, whose painting of Orvieto is now in the Tate in London. One tries to figure out from just where he did this painting but then of course he probably put various elements together in his studio in Rome where he used his on the spot sketches as inspiration.

The benches across the piazza invite you to sit and study the façade while swallows, and unfortunately pigeons, wheel or flutter around. It's also a great place for that favorite pastime of mine, as of many Orvietani and visitors: people-watching.

The façade of the cathedral has been compared to a page from an illuminated manuscript and truly it does look like a frontispiece that has been added on to the main building. But you should really first try and understand the plan of the building itself. Can you imagine discussions going on as to just what it was to be like? And the hundreds of workmen who had to be called in for this great undertaking? There are multitudes of ghosts milling around the square including stonecutters and masons who worked for years on the cathedral and are talking to each other in their French, German, or Lombard dialects. Between April 1347 and July 1348, there were 66 women on the payroll as well but they received only half the pay of their male colleagues. Can't you hear them complaining? After the plague, though, no more women. Not quite sure why.

Now, let's see whom we can corner. I'm sure that's Arnolfo di Cambio sitting on a bench over there, muttering to himself:

"A new cathedral! Since I was in Orvieto for the tomb of Cardinal de Braye, it seemed only logical that I should be asked for my ideas. They told me it was to be great and impressive, like Santa Maria Maggiore in Rome, so that the Orvietani too could say they had the most beautiful impressive church of all. True I am a sculptor, yet I am also an architect and designed the cathedral of Florence as well as Palazzo Vecchio and Santa Croce. I know, not everyone agrees with what I am about to say. But of course all of us, architects, sculptors, engineers, have to be well versed in all the arts. Take my successor, Lorenzo Maitani, who became capo maestro of the cathedral but was also overseer of bridges and civic buildings. I envisioned the church as a living organism, with six small semi-circular niches on each side, culminating in a great semi-circular apse. A wonderful rhythm. Too bad that the builders were in too great a hurry and that cracks developed in the apse."

And there's Lorenzo Maitani from Siena. As was normal in those days he was architect, engineer, sculptor. Let's ask him about his rather drastic solution:

"That semi-circular apse had to be torn down. It wouldn't work, not with the size of the building. So I had it replaced with a square tribune, and added buttresses at the sides just to make sure. I knew very well what had been going on in France with St. Denis and Abbot Suger. Now he was a true genius! The pointed arch meant that the weight of the vaulting no longer rested on the walls, which could easily be made higher. Then of course since I was named "universalis capid magister" or master mason, I also designed the façade. My drawings are still there in the Cathedral museum if you're interested. There are various perks to being capomastro – I was awarded citizenship of Orvieto, didn't have to pay taxes and was allowed to carry weapons. Like Arnolfo, I was also a sculptor, and bronze held no secrets for me. Aside from the panels with Genesis and the Last Judgment, what do you think of those four symbols of the Evangelists that look down so proudly from atop the piers? Which one do you like best? St. Matthew's winged man, St. John's eagle, St. Mark's winged lion, St. Luke's ox? I am particularly proud of the angels holding the curtains of Mary's baldachin. I'm told they are now in one of the papal palaces where you can see what a challenge it was to cast them."

"Thank you ever so much, Ser Lorenzo. You have told us so much about this incredible church. But before going in, let's take a closer look at the bas-relief panels and the stories they tell."

Aside from the façade as a whole, the most photographed features are the marble bas-reliefs on each pier. It would take hours to identify all the scenes, particularly in the second panel. And questions do come to mind as we look at them. The finest are undoubtedly the first and last panels, probably by Maitani himself. It has been suggested that they too, like the Madonna and angels over the main door, were heightened with color. Sculpture on the stone façade carving at that time often was, and a few instances can still be found where the impression of the whole tympanum is that of a colored carving, as in St. Foy in Conques in France. These Orvieto bas-reliefs are wonderful examples of story telling. Just see the angels commenting on each scene in the Genesis panel. Can you make out what they are whispering to each other?

Maitani's angels - Photo by Erika Bizzarri

"There's the Lord creating day and night, the waters with their fish. There's even a lobster there – do you see it? The birds that can fly like we can and the animals. What a variety! Wonder why He made them all so different. We may be angels but Adam certainly is handsome. Makes us want to touch him. The sculptor – not of course the Creator – must have seen classic Greek sculpture which came way before Christ appeared. Have you noticed how lovely Eve is as she floats out from

Adam's side? It's as if she were on a wave. And look up there, where the Lord is telling them not to eat the fruit of the tree of knowledge (which by the way looks like a fig tree) saying you know what will happen to you if you disobey. He really shouldn't have tempted them. Now why should Eve have been so curious? Are women generally more curious than men? Frankly we don't understand why it is all blamed on Eve. Seems to us Adam could have said no, but he didn't. So there. Like guilty children they are hiding under the bushes, but of course their Father will find them out. How sad! They really hadn't meant any harm. Guess the Lord was jealous that now they too would know things only He had known before."

Like some of the Greek nudes, there is something very tactile to Maitani's. Yet he based his depictions of the nude human body on Roman and Greek and perhaps Etruscan sculpture rather than on the living model. It wasn't till almost two hundred years later, with Signorelli, that artists studied the living (or dead in many cases) human body. Eve, for instance, floating from Adam's side could almost be a Roman Nereid born up by the waves. The figure of the Lord with his clinging drapery, typical of medieval French sculpture, is surely a sign that Maitani had been in touch with what was going on in France. Artists in those times traveled more than we think. We also know for instance that before painting his scenes with castles, Simone Martini traveled through the countryside, on horseback and with an assistant, so he could make sketches.

Have you noticed that Maitani's tree of knowledge is definitely not an apple tree? If you've studied art through the ages, you'll remember that fig leaves were also used in more prudish Victorian times to cover the private parts of figures, considered unfit for the eyes of innocent young women. That small scene way over in the corner with Adam and Eve cowering in the bushes, knowing they have done wrong, is a psychological masterpiece. I'm surprised Freud didn't have something to say about that. Up at the top is the story of Cain and Abel, and then the Liberal Arts. Freud might also have commented on the fourth panel with the Last Judgment, but I guess he was so struck by Signorelli's nudes, he overlooked this. The punishments meted out to the sinners are pretty much the same here as in Signorelli's frescoes in the

Cappella Nova. Maitani's dead, though, are shown rising not from the earth but from their coffins, which look like ancient Roman sarcophagi with that wavy-line decoration. The sinners are on Christ's left, the Blessed or Elect on His right.

In observing these bas-reliefs, a question does come to mind. Those bas-reliefs. The first and the last. Genesis and the Last Judgment. The beginning and the end. But how about the other two intervening panels? The third tells the story of Christ's life and that seems something you would expect. But the second panel is based on the tree of Jesse, depicting the kings of Israel, the genealogy of Christ. If you want to know what the individual scenes represent, there is a small guidebook by Giuseppe Mearilli that provides detailed information. It has been said that in stressing the humanity of Christ and Mary, the theme of the tree of Jesse is a refutation of the Cathar and Patarine heresy, which Orvieto seems to have been a hotbed of this heresy, according to which Christ was of one nature and fully divine. It was this, which Pope Urban IV was attempting to eliminate. While I had a vague idea of what Catharism was all about, our best bet is to turn to someone who was one himself. That gentleman over there, who is wearing the robes of a prior of the arts and guilds, looks as if he might help us out. They tell me his name is Domenico Tonicelli and that he was a Cathar, just the right sort of educated figure who can elucidate us.

"Yes, those were interesting years. We had a goodly contingent of Cathars here in Orvieto, merchants or moneylenders. But also artisans. We held public offices, as representatives of the people and as priors, and I myself was prior of the arts and guilds between 1255 and 1256. It wasn't until the Dominicans came in and called us heretics that our troubles began. Perhaps you're not quite clear on what we Cathars believed in. We felt that the spiritual and the material life should be separated. We wanted to build strong independent civic institutions in opposition to the ecclesiastical ones, which were so often corrupt. Among others who held public offices there was Martino, a prosperous merchant and consul. He came from a Cathar family and his sisters also married into a Cather family. We venerated the Cathar perfects, characterized by their extreme asceticism, and thereby thought of as trans-material angels, free from economic and political constraints. We were in agree-

ment with the "people", rather than the elite or the church, and what we wanted was a more powerful and independent city-state, to protect the common resources, mostly forests and pasturelands. The church should really have nothing to do with city politics. I suppose that may sound familiar to you from another time and country where separation of church and state was in your constitution.

With Urban IV resident in Orvieto from 1262 to 1274, a lot of jobs, meaning as many as 600, depended on the curia. Again that may sound familiar, for it is always the case when jobs depend on those in power."

All this of course made me look up the Cathars. Isn't that what life is all about – learning and following cues presented in daily experiences? So now I have a better idea of why they refused the idea of transubstantiation. I would have agreed with them as to its being symbolic, but I could not agree with the idea that the flesh was irredeemably evil. The spirit was of utmost importance to the Cathars and was described as being immaterial and sexless and that the world was a battleground between good, or spirit, and evil, or matter. The leaders, the perfects, remained chaste and avoided all foods that came from sexual union. They considered women equally capable of being spiritual leaders, thus undermining the concept of gender held by the Catholic Church. Obviously this did not go over well. Cathar beliefs refused the idea that Jesus was both human and divine, was fully God and fully man. For them He was of one nature, entirely divine since the human essence was inherently evil. Indeed, Pope Innocent III had sent his representative Pietro Parenzo to Orvieto to eliminate this heresy. You can see him in the Signorelli chapel in the Cathedral, with an ax in his head. Apparently the Orvietani were not convinced. Jesse's dream was therefore proof of the human nature of Christ. If you do look up Catharism you may be horrified at the lengths to which the Church went to try to eradicate the Cathars. But perhaps propaganda in the form of art would have been just as effective as torture and the inquisition. At least I like to think of it that way.

The Cathedral and its frescoes, names, the Miracle of Bolsena

The Cathedral is dedicated to Our Lady of the Assumption so it is natural that Mary should figure so largely with scenes ranging from her birth to her Assumption in heaven in the mosaics on the façade, as well as inside. The mosaics had been planned for in Maitani's drawings and those we see now date from the fourteenth to the seventeenth century, although they were so often restored it's hard to say what they looked like originally. Not so many years ago after a storm, the steps in front of the Cathedral were strewn with golden mosaic tesserae (those small bits of stone and glass used in making the designs) and a group of visiting Japanese tourists was enthusiastically picking them up. Things haven't changed all that much for I remember in 1955 when a friend and I visited Ravenna. Sant'Apollinare in Classe was under restoration but we convinced the custodian to let us enter after we promised to stay just in the nave. Upon leaving, he gave me several tesserae as, I suppose a sort of souvenir.

While there would be so many things to comment on once we're in the Cathedral, I'll have to limit myself to just a few. It certainly didn't always look as bare as it does now. Those small niches along the aisles still have the memory of what they originally held in the fourteenth century. The vintage photos in Sant'Agostino give us an idea of the changes that had taken place by the eighteenth century. They show you the church with the statues lined up along the columns, and the side altars with gilding and stuccoes and huge paintings, much of which done under the direction of Ippolito Scalza, before that regrettable, unfortunate decision in the late nineteenth century to return the interior to its "pristine condition".

As we move up to the apse, our attention centers on these two figures, with Gabriel speaking to Mary across the way. They seem to have a life of their own and you can feel them interact with the space around them. The heavenly messenger is enveloped in a tempestuous ocean of hollows and crests as he seems to have burst through the limits of the three dimensions. Mary is an earthbound human being who has just risen from her chair, frightened by this sudden apparition of an angel whirling down in the wind. *"What's going on here? And who are you?"* one can hear her saying, as she catches her breath, disconcerted by the appearance of this unexpected intruder. Francesco Mochi, the sculptor, is standing close by, hoping the Farnese duke will get him another commission after the Saint Philip and these two for the Cathedral of Orvieto. How young he looks! Not surprising, for he is only in his mid twenties. His figures of Mary and Gabriel (1605 and 1608), the word made flesh in the liturgy of the Eucharist, are where he had envisioned them, although in 1612 a cardinal bishop opposed their installation there, feeling that Mary in her revealing garment was too sensual. He may have been a priest but was evidently all too prone to feel the allure of the female form. Still in the nineteenth century, perhaps reflecting Victorian standards, Brockedon, in his guidebook, judged the Virgin, who was still at that time at the high altar, to be *"so little in consonance with the evangelical narrative, that, the beholder grows irreverent in thought whilst contemplating the figure ... there is too little of the humble Mary"*. (*Italy, Illustrated and Described*, in a Series of Views from Drawings by Stanfield, R.A., Roberts, R.A., Harding, Prout, Leitch, Brockedon, Barnard, etc.). Gabriel has been called the first truly Baroque sculpture. Somehow though, Mochi never followed up, and it was Bernini, his junior by eighteen years, who came to symbolize the Baroque with its drama and tension, and who overshadowed him.

While the figures of the other saints lining the aisle are not nearly as dramatic, the *Saint Thomas* by Ippolito Scalza merits careful scrutiny. On 22 May 1587, Scalza's St. Thomas was placed in the Cathedral with great fanfare, with trumpets and organs and the bells of all the churches in the city celebrating the event. Perhaps it shouldn't surprise us that the sculptor, in flesh and blood if one can say this of a ghost, is hovering nearby. Ippolito and Saint Thomas, we look at one and then the other, and the resemblance is indeed striking. An explanation does seem warranted as we tune in on Ippolito's words.

"Are you surprised that we look rather alike? Well, I'm an architect, and so was Saint Thomas. An architect and carpenter. See the try-square and compass he is holding? And the other architect's tools, the lead

holder and the astrolabe? He and I, both architects, so what's wrong with turning Thomas into a self-portrait? Don't know if I would have doubted the Resurrection though and would have had to actually touch Christ's wound to be convinced."

(If you're interested in following in the footsteps of Scalza, in addition to being master of the cathedral works, he was responsible for various palazzi in Orvieto as well as the façade of the town hall and the Pietà in the cathedral. He died in 1617 when he was 85, a truly venerable age at the time. In 2018, in celebration of 400 years of his passing, life-size silhouettes of St. Thomas/Scalza were set up outside buildings in which he had a hand. We'll pass by some of them in our wanderings, if they are still there and haven't been vandalized).

Of the other saints by various authors, the statue of *Saint Sebastian*, begun by Francesco Moschino, might be considered Ippolito Scalza's first Orvieto work. You'll generally see this martyr saint almost nude, with a loincloth around his hips, tied to a tree, his torso riddled with arrows. The small metal pieces on the body of the statue here are the remains of arrows. Together with Saint Roch, he was also known as a plague saint, as indicated by the wounds in his body.

They couldn't, however, do away with the alabaster windows, although parts of them were replaced by stained glass in the 1880s-90s. I love the golden hues when the sun shines in through these translucent alabaster panes.

If you have time, do look carefully at the frescoes in the apse by Ugolino di Prete Ilario (1370-84). Hmmm, wonder if Ugolino's father was a priest, for names can be very revealing. Take the following, which often don't tell you anything about the family but are more likely to tell you where the person was from or who the relatives were:

Antonio da San Gallo – original name Antonio Cordini – from a place called San Gallo.

Ugolino di Prete Ilario
(possibly his father was a priest named Ilario?)

Piero della Francesca (his mother's name was Francesca)

Ada del Maestro (last name Chiasso but known as del Maestro because her brother was the town's "maestro" or schoolteacher)

Or where you're from – Pisano or Romano

Caravaggio whose real name was Michelangelo Merisi, from Caravaggio a village close to Bergamo

Fra Angelico, obviously because of his angelic nature

Leonardo da Vinci, from a place called Vinci.

And then there are those that echo their time, such as Benito, Italia, Asia, and Eritrea during the Fascist era.

But back to these frescoes, which are rather like cartoon strips with only the speech bubbles missing. They're telling you the story of Anne and Joachim, of Mary and of Jesus. Anne and Joachim, remember, were Mary's parents, and Joachim's offering at the temple was refused because they had no children. Even though Anne was past her childbearing age, an angel visited her (and Joachim) and said she would have a child. There are lovely details in these frescoes and you're probably best off if you take binoculars. I love the cat and dog in the scene of the angel appearing to Saint Anne. In the interiors we note that the problem of storage was solved by having linen chests stowed away under the bed. Sheep are enclosed in a pen, with a dog barking at the announcing angels in the *Nativity* scene. Who's that dozing behind the shepherds in the *Adoration of the Shepherds*? None other than Joseph. I feel rather sorry for him since he always seems rather left out, even though it is truly to his credit that he accepted Jesus as his son.

Little details tell you of the cities of the time (certainly not the biblical times!) with the ubiquitous towers rising up behind the city walls and the grate in the ground-floor window, while a shade supported on a pole is in a window on the upper floor behind Elizabeth as she takes Mary's hand in hers. How charming the scene where Joseph is taking Mary home and the children are dancing in the street, with a man playing a lute and people watching from a balcony.

Ugolino had also been engaged for the frescoes in the chapel of the Miracle of Bolsena. He's standing over there in a corner, looking at them now, shaking his head for they are no longer really the way he had painted them.

"The colors and the brushstrokes aren't what they used to be but I suppose I'll just have to be satisfied with the stories they tell. I have been told that recently they were detached from the walls, and the underlying preparatory drawings are now in the museum. Perhaps they can tell you more about how I worked."

Since we don't have to worry about paying to enter the cathedral if all we want to do is meditate or pray in the chapel, why not go in and let the frescoes tell you the story? Of course Ugolino doesn't have to bother with the side entrance, or the ramp that provides access for pilgrims with wheelchairs. I wonder if any of them have been miraculously healed when they prayed here. Most pertinent is the story of the Miracle of Bolsena depicted on the right-hand wall. There is Peter of Prague bending over the altar as he says Mass in the church of Santa Cristina in Bolsena. He gazes incredulously at the Host from which drops of blood are falling on the Corporal or linen altar cloth. It is an answer to his anguished cry to God.

"Why dear God can't I believe? Why is it so hard for me to accept the fact that when I break bread at Mass it is transformed into the body of Christ and the wine becomes the chalice of His blood, the sacrifice our Lord Jesus Christ offered at the Cross? What have I done to make me so unworthy? There, now I am breaking the consecrated Host. God of my Fathers, enlighten me. The Host! Blood seems to be welling up from where I broke it, drops are falling on the linen altar cloth, the Corporal!

I bow my head in thanks, I feel faint. Truly a miracle to which those participating in the Mass bear witness. Quick, call the bishop so he too can confirm this miraculous event."

When Pope Urban IV, then resident in Orvieto, received the news, he immediately sent his bishop to verify and bring the Corporal to Orvieto. There is Urban IV himself down at the bridge over Rio Chiaro to receive this blood-stained cloth. When he then shows it to the people of Orvieto from his papal palace, the crowd erupts in cries of *"Miracle, Miracle."* In the houses in the background, a curtain is hanging from a horizontal pole – so that's what those stones with holes in them at the sides of the windows up high were for! Of course don't look for the Cathedral in this depiction of the city, for in 1264 it had not yet been built.

The pope exults. *"This is proof of transubstantiation. It shall be celebrated in a solemn feast day, Corpus Domini, and Thomas Aquinas shall write the services for the day. After all Thomas is teaching at San Domenico and he is the perfect person to do so."*

Yet this was only one of those miracles that proved the pope's belief, for there was also one in Belgium where a nun had a similar experience. And since we are sitting here with nothing particular to do, we can pass the time and keep out of the July sun by reading the stories of the other frescoes, most of which have to do with the Eucharist and the significance of transubstantiation, the transformation of the bread and wine of the Mass into the actual body and blood of Christ. There is the story of the Crusaders captured by the Saracens who permit the priest to perform Mass. When the Child appears miraculously in the Host, they free their prisoners and are converted. There's a little Jewish boy who takes communion with his Christian play fellows and whose father, irate is too mild a description, with an evil smirk on his face, thrusts the child into a flaming oven. Three days later however the boy is taken out, safe and sound, thanks to the intervention of the Virgin. Note the boy is dressed in yellow, a sign that he was Jewish. Elsewhere I have discussed the Jews and their place in contemporary society. If you really want to know more about the frescoes, which were meant to confirm belief in the doctrine of transubstantiation, there is a small guide to the Chapel (in English) by Catherine Harding (University of Victoria).

The question sometimes arises as to what happened to Peter of Prague, since at least in Orvieto he seems to disappear from the scene. He wasn't just an ordinary priest but seems to have been an important diplomat, involved in getting Urban IV to agree to a military expedition in Lithuania, still a pagan land, by the Bohemian king.

Then there is that large panel painting where Mary is shown sheltering people under her cloak – the men on her right, the women on her left. Most of them are looking at Mary, but a few are looking straight out at us, as if to invite us in. It's called the *Madonna of the Raccommandati* (quite fitting for Italy where you generally need someone to recommend you when looking for a job or an apartment), or the *Madonna of Mercy*. The artist was Lippo Memmi, Simone Martini's brother-in-law. Artists too do tend to stick together.

Ippolito Scalza – sixty years dedicated to the Cathedral, Gentile da Fabriano and pastries

Aside from Signorelli, one of the most important personalities in the construction of the Cathedral and its embellishment was Ippolito Scalza, whom we have already met. He was a true Orvietano and there was nothing "formal" about his relationship with the cathedral authorities of the Opera del Duomo, for he did not hesitate to tell them what he thought. To tell the truth he did have things to complain about:

"You know sixty years of my life I gave to the cathedral works. Took me quite a while though to be appreciated – and all because I was born here in Orvieto. Others who came from outside had it better – take Lorenzo Maitani, called in to repair the damages to the apse when the cathedral was under construction. Now he was from Siena, a "foreigner"

and therefore to be appreciated. Same can be said for Raffaelo da Montelupo. I did get my say, however, with the authorities of the Opera. Told them what I thought, made suggestions. And they generally listened to me – except for paying me my due. Even as late as 1567 I had to petition them for the post of capo maestro. I also told them that since the organ had to be redone, I would see to the ornaments as well as the tuning, so they wouldn't have to bring in outsiders. I was eventually named capo maestro but not at the salary previously assigned Montelupo. Took thirteen years to get that. Not quite fair, I'd say. As time passed I finally put the finishing touches on the facade, thanks also to the fact that the clerics didn't have all that much say – yes, quite an unusual situation, but then in 1421, thanks to Pope Martin V, the Opera became a communal organism almost totally free from any ecclesiastical presence."

The fact that the Cathedral fell under the jurisdiction of the civic authorities and not of the Church was particularly important.

"In my humble opinion, the large marble Pietà is my masterpiece. A single block of marble! Getting the material for the building of the cathedral to the top of the cliff was never easy. Basalt and travertine were local stones but when it comes to the marble for the statues, all I can say is try and imagine you're a bug perched on a block of marble hoping to get from the Carrara quarries to Orvieto. Over sea and land, with pirates and the Turks and the French armies lying in wait. The first loads did not arrive until 1556."

"I had already finished a St. Sebastian begun by Francesco Moschino. I find a payment document of 1573 noting that a shop assistant had acquired a length of linen to drape around Sebastian's hips quite amusing. All the fault of Carlo Borromini and the Council of Trent. Nudity in churches? But we were born naked and the saints certainly didn't care whether they had on the latest fashions or not."

Evidently though some of us still think there's something shameful about the naked human body – take what happened in 2016 when the visiting president of Iran passed through the Capitoline Museum in Rome on his way to a meeting. Oh dear, someone thought, we'd better not take a chance on offending him! So they not only draped the ancient nude statues but hid them behind boxes. And even more recently, photos of the nude Neptune statue on the Bologna fountain were removed from Facebook as being too explicitly sexual.

"Finally though in 1570 I was commissioned to sculpt a Pietà, *a statue that means more to me than anything else. I imagine you can see reminiscences of Michelangelo in the way the figure of Christ lies on his mother's lap, and how she doesn't actually touch her son's body directly. Then I added two other figures, Mary Magdalene and Joseph of Arimathea. I have been trying for years to get the Opera to give my* Pietà *a proper place of its own in the cathedral, for it is after all a source of income for the Opera, encouraging offerings by the faithful"*

We'll be back but as we exit, there's one more thing to catch our attention.

There's a painting to our right just before we open that door to the present. It's by Gentile da Fabriano, who met with the bishop in 1425 to discuss the fresco. The Cathedral archives contain a bill for pastries – sweets for Gentile – so they evidently had a reception for him.

Gentile da Fabriano. What a lovely name. Again, Gentile was from Fabriano. If you want his full name it was Gentile di Niccolò di Giovanni di Massio – oh dear here we go back several generations.

"Delighted, Monsignor. These pastries are delicious. I should be able to finish that fresco of Mary and Jesus in about a month. And I'll put an angel over to her left – a wisp of a figure, just a breath, for of course angels are not flesh and blood and could hardly be painted as if they were."

Although now looking at his fresco, Gentile wonders why it had to be cut down. True, a figure of St. Catherine in oil had been added in the 16th century, fortunately removed in the restorations of the 1980s.

"I don't quite understand why my fresco of the Madonna and Child had to be altered. I'm relieved that that figure of St. Catherine was removed – she was, I hate to say it, rather ugly and covered my aerial angel. I can perhaps see that the Opera wanted to align the vertical axis of the

fresco with the window above, but it was a pretty drastic solution to cut the composition down at the left. Yet I am glad that the Opera wanted to integrate the cathedral's past into a new vision for the side aisles. Does it bother you in looking at it now that it's not all perfectly aligned? Perhaps you're also aware that the Child is so much more a baby than in earlier depictions. And note that shadows in the painting are cast with light coming from the left – where there really is a window."

And then we push the door, and are back out in the 21st century, leaving the 14th century behind us.

World War II and the saving of Orvieto

Maybe this is the moment to tell you a story that has to do with much more recent history. Although you may not remember those years, your parents or grandparents would. We're going back to 1944. June 14, 1944. World War II with Germany and Italy against the Allies, in particular Great Britain, the United States, Russia and France, who were advancing from the south. Italy had realized that it was over and had signed the peace treaty, with Mussolini fleeing north. The Germans however were still hanging on, and Orvieto was one of their strongholds. Machine gun emplacements had been set up along the edge of the cliff, including not far from the cathedral. The commander at the time, Luftwaffe Oberstleutnant Alfred Lersen, and Monsignor Pieri, bishop of Orvieto, had struck up a friendship since they shared a love of art and music. There they are, going into the Cathedral, conversing in Latin (hopefully you'll remember enough to follow their conversation), as they shut the doors and ask the organist to play some Bach for them.

Fifty years later in 1994, the 50th anniversary of the treaty of peace that ended Italian participation in World War II, the mayor of Orvieto received a letter from a Major Heseltine in Great Britain. There weren't all that many expats or people who knew English in Orvieto at the time, and since I had occasionally helped the mayor when the occasion arose, I was given the letter to translate. It read as follows:

To the Mayor of Orvieto
From Major R. Heseltine M.C. (3rd the Kings own Hussars)

Greetings.
I have the honour to address the Mayor of Orvieto, regrettably in English, for which I must apologise.

Fifty years ago on the 14th of June 1944, I was in command of the leading squadron of British tanks approaching Orvieto from Viterbo.
That city had suffered devastation and your citizens must have feared like treatment.

But when I could see Orvieto far in the distance, standing high on its island of rock, my forward troop reported a German Volkswagen approaching flying a white flag.

I therefore ordered the troop officer to intercept and bring them to me. They were a German Oberleutnant and his driver bearing a message from their commander. I cannot remember the wording, but in effect it declared there were no Germans in or around the city and that on account of the historic beauty of Orvieto, the area German commander proposed that with the agreement of the Allied command they jointly declare Orvieto an open city.

I therefore despatched the envoy under escort to the higher authority, where it was readily agreed.

A few hours later, my squadron now in reserve, was resting below the rock near the road entry up into the city. With my second in command we two entered the town in a jeep. It was like a dead city, everyone was in hiding.

As we clattered through the narrow empty streets we suddenly emerged into the piazza and stopping beheld in astonishment the facade of your wonderful Cathedral, sure one of the most sublime sights in all the world.

But as we sat there transfixed in admiration, someone noticed our uniform, and then the whole town came running and engulfed us in rejoicing.

Sadly two days later, when again in the lead on the road to Città della Pieve, near the village of Ficule my leading troop was ambushed and Cpt. Howard Riley killed. He lies in a little cemetery in the shadow of your beautiful city.

I though as a participant you might be interested in this account of the liberation of Orvieto on its fiftieth anniversary.

Although the Germans chose not to defend Orvieto, the advancing Allies would not have known this, so might well have bombed and shelled the city.

That Orvieto was left untouched was due to the initiative of the German general. And I have often wondered if he had returned to Orvieto in happier days. But perhaps he did not survive the war.

With Sincerity
Richard Heseltine
March 21st 1994
'Centuries'
Assington
Sudbury
Suffolk C010 5LW
England

In 1996 Major Heseltine returned to Orvieto, and stood at the corner of the square, right where Marino's shop is now, and relived that moment. In 1944 he had come up, not along Via Maitani opposite the Cathedral, but up Via Duomo. There are still some around who remember that day. They had been taking refuge in the caves when the Allies arrived and the soldiers handed out chocolate and candy to the children.

Later still, Manfred Lersen, Alfred Lersen's son, came to Orvieto, where he discovered a hitherto unknown aspect of his father, who had rarely spoken of his war experiences at home. Since then friendships have been formed and Orvieto now hopes to celebrate June 14th every year, the day that Orvieto was declared an Open City and saved from destruction. Manfred also donated to the City the typewriter on which the request for declaring Orvieto an Open City was written. 2019. The seventy-fifth anniversary of Orvieto Open City. Celebrations were called for. David Zarko offered to write a play and the expats, mostly English-speaking members, got together to contribute the money for the staging. The result was *Colloquia*, presented in English and Italian, translated by Andrea Brugnera. It was based on real events, as narrated by Sandro Bassetti in his book on *Orvieto Città Aperta*, and imagined what might have gone on between the German commander and the bishop of Orvieto at the time. For the occasion the German commander's son and family came from Meissen, two granddaughters of Major Heseltine, who was the first of the Allies to arrive in Orvieto, came from England, the Orvietani rallied, in particular Montanucci and the Michelangelis. The Germans brought with them a commemorative plaque that is now located on the left wall of Palazzo Soliano, across from the Cathedral.

I like to think of other moments when "enemy armies" had camped at the base of the cliff to starve the inhabitants into surrender. The Romans did so in the third century BC. In the two years of their siege their soldiers had time to loot the Etruscan tombs and take whatever gold they could find, before the Etruscans finally surrendered in 264 BC. Then in the sixth century Belisarius camped at the base of the cliff and starved the Goths, who had taken over the city, into surrender.

Subsequently Orvieto watched the invading troops of Charles V pass by in the valley on their way to Rome, where they wreaked havoc in what is known as the Sack of Rome. For fear of further sieges, Clement VII had Saint Patrick's Well begun in 1527 after the sack of Rome. In a sense the story of Orvieto, with its continuous warfare and limited periods of peace, is no different from the larger world of today.

Signorelli and the End of the World

So far we haven't really taken a good look at what most consider the leading attraction of Orvieto, aside from the Cathedral itself. There are frescoes in the apse, and we have looked at those as well as attempting to understand the stories told in the chapel of the Corporal. What visitors then and now, including Michelangelo, have been most enthusiastic about though are those in the Cappella Nuova. It's time we too let ourselves be drawn into that catastrophic world. Best to let the protagonists tell us a bit, beginning with Luca Signorelli.

"His" chapel is in the space created by Maitani's buttresses. It was later home to a miraculous icon of Mary and the infant Christ dated to around 1200. I suppose I shouldn't say it was Signorelli's chapel since it had been begun by Fra Angelico and the Monaldeschi coat of arms is in the corners of the vault section with the Choir of Virgins. When it was decided that two members of opposing Monaldeschi families be joined in marriage so as to end the family bickering, 100 florins were donated for the completion of the frescoes, although there were other bequests throughout the years. Guess that's often the fate of the patrons – what they sponsored, then got known by the artist's name. The decoration of the chapel was however controlled and paid for by the Opera del Duomo. Their symbol is at the top of the triumphal arch framing the entrance portal – OPSM or Opera Pia Santa Maria. They first entrusted Fra Angelico, the Dominican friar, with the decoration of the chapel. He, however, only did the two vault sections with the judging Christ and the Prophets, in a sort of realm outside time. Some say he had accepted the commitment in Orvieto in June of 1447 to get away from the heat of a Roman summer. He was called back to Rome several months later, where he painted several frescoes for Nicholas V, and work in Orvieto came to a halt. When the whole chapel was being restored (1989-1996), one could go up on the scaffolding and see his work up close. The minuteness of his brushwork, as if he expected the viewer to be no more than several feet away, was breathtaking. After all, Fra Angelico was painting for God, not for the mortals down below. Time passed. Various other painters were approached and either did a few minor portions, or never kept their promises. Then finally, maybe also because the money had been found, Luca Signorelli of Cortona was "interviewed" for the job and asked to do a trial two sections of the vault. The Opera approved of what he had done and the contract was stipulated. We still have it in the Cathedral Archives. Let's see what Luca has to say.

There he is, to one side of the scene with the Antichrist, observing his work. He's only an onlooker, not part of that collage of events he's put together. A mature handsome figure, a greatcloak enveloping his body, with Fra Angelico right behind him. Indeed, Vasari, that gossipy biographer of the artists of his time, said that Signorelli liked to dress well. The subject was the *End of the World*, already approved for Fra Angelico. And that is the story the frescoes over the entrance tell us, the end of the world according to the predictions of the astrologers of the time. The sun and moon are in the sky together, statues are falling from their pedestals and huge waves or tsunamis rise up in the background. Fire and brimstone are hailing down from the sky and men and women with babes in their arms are vainly trying to flee the flames licking up around them. Let's ask Luca about his contract, which is still there in the archives.

"The opera asked me to do two trial vault sections before deciding to take me on, even though I was already "the most famous painter in all of Italy" as some documents say, and at work in Monte Oliveto. Well they did decide in my favor and the contract states that they will see to the scaffolding and the plaster. There is to be lodging for two, even though my assistants will be more than two. I also insisted on including enough grain for my assistants, and of course those 1000 liters of golden Orvieto wine. As usual, I agreed to do the heads and hands of the fig-

ures, but my assistants could take care of the drapery and background. Normal procedure. And as for the colors, well, lapis lazuli blue is really expensive so the Opera has to see to that, as well as the gold. Of course I was also to be paid for my labors, paints, designs and cartoons to the tune of 575 ducats."

Cartoons in art-historical language refer to the full-size preparatory drawings the artists made before actually painting their fresco. The outlines were then either traced onto the wet plaster with a stylus or pounced with charcoal through small holes in the drawing. Cartoons were also used as indications for the craftsmen in weaving tapestries, and were not of the Mickey Mouse or Donald Duck type most of us are acquainted with.

"For the vaults I could simply follow Fra Angelico's example, with what you would now describe as group photographs. But faced with that vast expanse of white walls, I had to do something else. My idea was to construct a continuity of the architecture of the space and have the episodes unroll like scenes on a stage. The one you should look at first, a true collage of episodes, skittering from one moment in the present to another, is the one over to your left upon entering. That figure standing on a Roman pedestal, with the devil whispering in his ear, is none other than the Antichrist who was to precede the End, passing himself off as the Messiah – a false messiah he was indeed. I did make him handsome, like Christ, but with an evil cast to his features. I rather envisioned him as resembling Savonarola, that fanatic friar in Florence who had been hanged and burned just before I started my work here, or the Turkish sultan, for after all one of the signs of the End was the advance of the Infidels from the East. He's surrounded by figures of the past and present, Dante, Petrarch, a Monaldeschi, and, you would never guess who – that figure in yellow with a square white neckline who has been identified as Christopher Columbus. Check the dates. When was America discovered? When were these scenes painted? You can't say I wasn't aware of what was going on in the world. And that man with a beret and a yellow cloak paying out money to a woman (or is it a man?) is a Jewish moneylender. Then of course the time was rife with signs of heavenly displeasure. Take the Black Death for instance which came back in cycles although the worst epidemic was in 1348, when in larger cities like

Florence 70% of the population died. I did use a sort of pattern book of poses and you can find figures that resemble each other in many of these scenes. Those monks surrounding a Dominican friar – here we have the Dominicans again – are discussing the apocalyptic texts, in particular Daniel 12. Note how St. Vincent Ferrer in the center is counting the days on his fingers. Up there on the left, the Antichrist attempts to ascend to Heaven. He does after all believe himself to be the new Messiah, but is hurled down by one of the archangels. That church, or temple, in the background, with ominous black figures hovering around it, follows the precise dictates of that great architect, Alberti, since it is central plan, with three steps leading up and with no stained glass windows that might distract the congregation."

Before moving on to the *Resurrection of the Flesh* across the way, don't you find that group in the foreground right to the left of the entrance arch, whose bodies are either receding into space or moving out towards you, fascinating? Perspective! One of the guiding interests of the Renaissance. And the feeling of panic and impossibility of flight is given by the way in which the space seems to implode!
Luca interrupts our admiration of his skill in depicting these three-dimensional bodies and directs our attention to the large scenes on the right-hand wall. He does seem to be quite proud of what he's done here.

"What better chance to show my knowledge of the human figure than in a resurrection scene. Nude bodies. Certainly not everyone, particularly if faint of heart, would want to strip a cadaver down to the bones, to see how the muscles were attached to each other. But such was our thirst of knowledge that we did. Leonardo and Michelangelo and other artists. I used the body of my son, who had just died, as model for the figure of the dead Christ in my Lamentation in the niche in the Cappella Nova. You say I might not have ever seen a skeleton as such. You are probably right but what interested me were the muscles and in this most theatrical of scenes, the Resurrection of the Flesh, I had a chance to show off my skill. Angels on high are blowing their trumpets as the dead take on flesh and rise from their graves. Even if my skeletons are not all that lifelike – can one use that word for skeletons? – don't you love that group peering out from behind the arch on the right?"

"I think though what fascinated me most, what was the greatest challenge, and what I enjoyed most for it let my imagination run riot, was the scene with the Damned. It is pure theater with a tangle of bodies, no way of extricating oneself, no way of getting a breath of fresh air. And I could put anyone who had crossed me there. There's a blonde woman, being carried down to Hell piggyback on a flying devil. She should never have played around with my emotions. Of course others have always put people they dislike into Hell – be they popes or bishops or their mistresses. You ask why the devils are blue and green. I was fortunate enough to see some ancient tomb paintings where the entrance to the netherworld was guarded by blue and green demons. Then of course when I dissected cadavers, depending on how long it took, their flesh might start to putrefy."

"You think we always followed our original sketches? Of course we were painting on wet plaster so once it was dry, we couldn't change things. But we didn't necessarily have to follow the indications of the sinopia, and signs that I changed my mind about the position of an arm or leg are easy to see. Even if the painting was done and dry, there was always a but and we could overpaint. That woman in the foreground, with a devil pulling with all his might on something absolutely invisible, well there was once a thong that went around her neck. Unfortunately too enthusiastic overcleaning eliminated that. You'd never guess what one of the best ways to take the soot and dirt off a picture was. If you've ever been at a dinner party and get a bit bored waiting for the next course, I'll bet you toyed with a piece of bread, kneading it into a ball. You're right, it turns sort of grey because it takes the dirt off your fingers. So it would also take the dirt off a fresco, without damaging what was underneath. Now look at the man kneeling on one leg next to that poor lady lying on the ground. Can you see that shadow across his thigh? And further up there's another shadow across his groin. Well, those are the ghostly traces of a serpent that was biting his private parts. Oh yes, artists, and priests, always loved these sexual tortures. The sinners are being sucked into a vortex of flames and in the scenes to the right of the altar we see them being herded along the river Styx to whatever circle they have been condemned. One thing I'll bet practically no one ever notices is that tondo in the window niche just above the altar. What a shame they ruined my frescoes there when they put in that baroque altar in the early 18th century. There's a suspended egg in that tondo – and eggs signify regeneration. In the early 1470s my master Piero della Francesca also put one in his famous painting known as the Brera Altarpiece where an egg is hanging in a sort of shell-like semi-dome above the Virgin enthroned."

"The fact that Mary, in the vault section with the Apostles, looks as if she were pregnant might also need to be explained. It is certainly not by chance, for across from us is the chapel of the Miracle of Bolsena, where the bread and wine became the Body and Blood of Christ. And between these chapels, in the apse, is the altar where this miracle is celebrated in the Eucharist. So what we have here with Mary is the Word becoming Flesh."

What a description Luca has given us! So perhaps a mention of the lower tier, the zoccolo, is also in order. Unlike the lunettes, which take place in our time and space, this register is the world before our time. It was meant to be studied in detail and we have portraits of ancient Greek philosophers and poets as well as Dante, together with monochrome tondos of scenes pertaining to civic discord and personal salvation. They are from the *Divine Comedy* and Ovid's *Metamorphosis*, among others. If you do have the time I'm sure you can find a guidebook to explain each individual picture.

Please do note that all the scenes to the left of the judging Christ deal with murder and mayhem (remember in Italian the word for left is *sinistra*, like our English sinister), while scenes of peace and prosperity are on Christ's right. You'll find this wherever you have a judging Christ – the blessed on his right, the damned on his left.

And those scrolling plant decorations with animals and men in the midst? Again history comes to the fore. You probably know that Nero was anything but a popular emperor and that when he died, his palace was buried and his lake, later to become the site of the coliseum, was filled in. Well, it was at this time in the Renaissance that Nero's Golden House was rediscovered but to get into the rooms, you had to go underground, into caves, or grottoes. Some were decorated with this type of scroll decoration, which then became known as grotesques, from the word grotto. Raphael was also quite taken with these designs. They were the inspiration behind the motif known as Raphaelesque you'll find on some of the ceramics in the shops on Via Duomo.

With reference to Signorelli, someone might have mentioned Freud and the fact that, after a visit to Orvieto, he couldn't remember the name of the artist who did the frescoes in the cathedral. It seems to have been this that led to his discovery of repression in his theories on psychoanalysis and the Oedipus complex. A plaque has recently been put up on the Corso in what was then the Albergo delle Belle Arti, and is now Palazzo Bisenzi, where he stayed. One never knows how what you see today will have an impact on what you experience tomorrow.

Cathedral Museum and Henry VIII

If we really want to get an idea of what art was produced throughout the centuries, the Cathedral Museum known as MODO is a must. Maybe you've had your fill of museums. But not if you begin asking yourselves what, when and why. Besides which the statue of Mary once over the main entrance is there. Let me point out just a few things and give you a few "pushes" to get you going. As you start through the tunnel that runs along from one side of the cathedral to the other, there are indications that take you to the museum proper. The route leads through a room with early fresco fragments that don't seem all that interesting to us non-specialists. As we move out into the courtyard, those steps going up to the main part of the museum seem to be saying: come on, what's up here is really fabulous. This then is what the papal palace was like, although here too there were frescoes. Still even though most of them are gone, we can picture what it was like in the 13th-14th century. Except – yes, except if we move forward in time, to the sixteenth century, things are not what you would expect them to be. Was it here that Henry VIII's ambassadors came to ask the pope to annul his marriage to Catherine so he could marry Anne Boleyn? A palace that at the time had rain leaking in the roof and with furniture that wasn't worth a hoot, as the English ambassadors Gardiner and Foxe reported? Or it might have been the bishop's palace. A description of their journey and arrival in Orvieto gives us an idea of the times. (Chapter 10, History of the Reformation, vol. 5 HRSCV5 8022, 23, 24):

Fox and Gardiner, after a gracious reception at Paris (23rd February) by Francis I, arrived at Orvieto on the 20th of March, after many perils, and with their dress in such disorder, that no one could have taken them for ambassadors of Henry VIII. "What a city!" they exclaimed, as they passed through its streets; "what ruins, what misery! It is indeed truly called Orvieto (urbs vetus)!" The state of the town gave them no very grand idea of the state of the popedom, and they imagined that with a pontiff so poorly lodged, their negotiation could not be otherwise than easy. "I give you my house," said Da Casale, to whom they went, "my room and my own bed;" and as they made some objections, he added: "It is not possible to lodge you elsewhere; I have even been forced to borrow what was necessary to receive you."

Da Casale, pressing them to change their clothes, which were still dripping (they had just crossed a river on their mules), they replied, that being obliged to travel post, they had not been able to bring a change of raiment. "Alas!" said Casale, "what is to be done? there are few persons in Orvieto who have more garments than one; even the shopkeepers have no cloth for sale; this town is quite a prison. People say the pope is at liberty here. A pretty liberty indeed! Want, impure air, wretched lodging, and a thousand other inconveniences, keep the holy father closer than when he was in the Castle of St. Angelo. Accordingly, he told me the other day, it was better to be in captivity at Rome than at Liberty here." In two days, however, they managed to procure some new clothing; and being now in a condition to show themselves, Henry's agents were admitted to an after-dinner audience on Monday the 22nd of March (1528). Da Casale conducted them to an old building in ruins. "This is where his holiness lives," he said. They looked at one another with astonishment, and crossing the rubbish lying about, passed through three chambers whose ceilings had fallen in, whose windows were curtainless, and in which thirty persons, "riff-raff, were standing against the bare walls for a garnishment." This was the pope's court."

Whatever the case, at the time the statue of the Madonna with six angels drawing aside the curtains of the baldachin would have been over the main entrance to the cathedral, where it has now been replaced by a copy. Why a copy? True, the air in Orvieto isn't nearly as polluted as in Florence where practically all the marble statues in buildings along the street are now copies, since the exhaust from cars has gradually eaten away the outer layers of the stone. But we do have pigeons, even if attempts are made to keep them at a due distance by putting in sonic deterrents. That's what those clicks you hear are as you try to identify the scenes in the golden mosaics on the façade. The marble Madonna is by an unidentified Umbrian-Sienese sculptor, and the six bronze angels are probably by Maitani, the architect who was master of the cathedral works. The group dates to between 1325 and 1330. I like to imagine the figures when they were first put up, brilliantly colored.

Of course Greek (and Etruscan) statues were also once colored and our idea of them as white marble is quite unreal. Look carefully and you can see traces of color on their shoes as well as on the borders of Mary's cloak. Maitani's angels are masterpieces of casting and the iron core in the figures that almost seem to be dancing is quite visible. There were gold and glass decorations and the "sky" of the baldachin was blue. Very simply I can say I love the Madonna and the purity of her profile. It does help to know that the rather clumsy right forearm and the arms of the Child are later restorations and not the fault of the unknown sculptor of the original.

In the large room to our right be sure to take a good look at the drawings on the walls – they are the sinopias, or preparatory designs, for the frescoes, done with a red earth from Sinop in Turkey. Once the sponsors had given their OK and the artists were ready to begin the final version, fresh plaster was applied but only in patches large enough to be painted in a single day while the plaster was still wet. You're probably wondering how these underlying drawings got here, if they had been covered over with plaster. Most of them are from the frescoes in the chapel of the Miracle of Bolsena, which are still in place on the walls. The answer is that a fresco can be removed from the wall by gluing a sort of netting on it and with an energetic yank, off it comes. Sounds incredible but that's how it's done. The layer underneath is then revealed and sometimes that too can be removed, giving us an insight into the workings of the artist's mind. I often like the sinopias better than the finished fresco for they also show you how the artist experimented with different compositions or even changed his mind as he was working.

Striking examples of this kind of restoration are the frescoes on the vault of the apse, or tribune as it's often called. They were almost falling to pieces, what with previous attempts at restoration using clamps and injections of plaster and such. The only thing to do after restoring what could be restored was to remove them. But they were enormous, as large as your living room carpet. They did it though, ripping the top layer of plaster off and rolling the frescoes up on huge cylinders, before preparing a new backing and returning them to the original site. I shudder to think of it.

Every object in the museum deserves a careful study but since there's a very good catalog of the museum online, in English, just a note on my favorites. In the room with sculpture there are two small unfinished statues where you can visualize the sculptor chipping away at the marble and can even identify the types of chisels used. And that over-life-size blessing Christ! Wonder where they found a pear tree of that size. *The Madonna Enthroned* attributed to Coppo di Marcovaldo, with the gold patterning of the folds of her garment in what is known as Byzantine style, is so unlike most of the paintings we've encountered so far. She looks so serious and there is something mesmerizing about her gaze. She is said to know what the future holds for her son and that's nothing to be happy about. Don't turn around now, but there's Coppo trailing us as he tells us how he was commissioned to do this Madonna. He does have a beautiful Tuscan lilt to his speech.

"In 1261 I was fighting on the side of the Florentine Guelphs in the battle of Montaperti, a terrible battle where the river was said to have turned red with the blood of those massacred. I was captured, although I still don't know why I wasn't killed, and taken to Siena. Since I was a painter and art was important to the Sienese, they had me paint a Madonna and Child for their Servite church. The one you see here also used to be in the Servite church in Orvieto and some say it's not by me. You'll have to decide. Don't you like the way the Madonna inclines her

head to her Son and seems to envelop him with her arms?"

Along the corridor, I always linger a moment in front of the wooden Annunciation, with a sweet accepting Mary. How different from Mochi's version it is. Artists, or the donors, had their own ideas of what Mary's emotional response would have been. Just think about it. There you are quietly reading a book and suddenly a winged figure appears out of nowhere. Sometimes she is shown surprised, sometimes frightened, or, as here, unquestioning. I love one version in San Galgano near Siena where she is hanging on to a column for dear life at the appearance of Gabriel. This was however only in the preliminary drawing in the sinopia, for evidently it was too unorthodox for those who had commissioned the fresco, which was then done in a more traditional pose.

The polyptych or multi-panel altar painting by Simone Martini (ca. 1324) was painted for the church of S. Domenico. The Dominicans seem to have been about everywhere in Orvieto! The painting gives you a chance to test your knowledge of the saints by identifying their attributes: Mary Magdalene with her ointment jar, Dominic in Dominican garb and holding a lily, Peter with a key, and Paul with a book and sword. You'll note that three saints are looking to their left, towards Mary, but only one is on the other side, looking to his right. Obviously there should have been two other saints to make it three on each side. The donor, the tiny bishop below Mary Magdalene's hands, is a Monaldeschi. There's another similar polyptych, complete this time but with only four saints, in Boston in the Isabella Stewart Gardner Museum, in the acquisition of which Bernard Berenson had a hand. For a while I worked at his villa at I Tatti, as secretary to BB, or rather to his librarian, Nicky Mariano, since he was already in his 90s and spent most of the time in bed. While Berenson was responsible for reviving interest in Italian Renaissance art, he was also a shrewd businessman, spiriting many paintings out of Italy and making enormous profits at the same time.

Fast forward to the last room (but first stop a minute to admire the rich garments of Signorelli's large *Mary Magdalene* with her usual jar of ointment. She was commissioned by the city after she was promoted patron of Orvieto and originally was in the Signorelli chapel). A sort of identifying mark of Signorelli's is the way he treats hands. They look rather like jointed wooden artist's models. It's things like this that help tell you who the artist of an unknown painting was. Further on, the large panel paintings, most over thirteen feet high, were once in the Cathedral over the altars in the niches along the aisle or on the counter-façade. In the 19th century when it was decided to return the Cathedral to its "pristine condition", these paintings and the altars, dating mostly to the 16th-17th centuries, were removed. The one I want you to look at in particular is *The Birth of the Virgin* by Cesare Nebbia (1582). It was commissioned by Sforza Monaldeschi and the birth is shown taking place in their palazzo, which still exists and is not far from the church of San Francesco. Wouldn't you say they were being a bit exhibitionistic? The palazzo later became the art institute, the art high school.

In the foreground, the donors, Sforza Monaldeschi and his wife and daughter, by now just as large as the other figures and saints in the scene, are observing and eavesdropping as the women chatter away and prepare the bath for the newborn infant. *"Careful, be sure the water isn't too hot. The swaddling band is ready too. Guess Madonna Anna had a fairly easy birth despite her age. After all she never expected to have a child on in years like this. Surely she can have some of that chicken broth – and maybe even eat a bit of chicken. Is that Joachim up there waiting in the background, receiving two doves, offerings for the temple? This time he won't be turned away."* Quite true, poor Joachim was turned away from the temple, also shown in the frescoes in the apse of the Duomo, because they didn't have any children and that was interpreted as a sign that God was not on their side.

I have two strips of swaddling cloths, each about 3 yards long, together with the baptismal dresses of my sons, in what was once called a hope chest and versions of which appear in frescoes and paintings, often stowed away under a bed. The bands came down from my in-laws, although by the time my sons were born no one used them any more.

In case you're wondering, it has been suggested that the woman in blue in the doorway might be a premonition of Mary as mother of Jesus.

Before leaving be sure to take a look at the Albèri library where the silver and enamel reliquary, which looks rather like a miniature Duomo and was originally made in the fourteenth century for the miraculous altar cloth, is now housed. The library, annexed to the cathedral, is a rare example of joint library and cathedral. Bishop Albèri left his collection of manuscripts and incunabula or books printed before 1501 to the Cathedral. The frescoes, dedicated to the disciplines found in the library itself and contemporary with what Signorelli was doing in the Cappella Nova, have been restored. If you don't have all that much time, do at least look at the monkey wearing eyeglasses on the embrasure of the last window in the southwest corner. He is reading an open book with the words *Legere et non intelligere est negligere*. (In other words if you don't understand what you are reading, you might as well not read at all).

As we leave the museum and wander out into the real world where a late afternoon breeze is coming around the corner, there's a certain melancholy in the air. We've seen so many things and there are so many that we haven't seen. Let's take a cue from our little monkey friend. When we go elsewhere, unless we are open, receptive, to a world that has new things to tell us, we might as well not go anywhere, but just stay home.

Museo MODO, Libreria Albèri (copyright Opera del Duomo di Orvieto)

What Orvieto is for me

I've been in Orvieto almost 60 years, I call it home, but I still try to see it with fresh eyes, to remain alive to its distinctive characteristics, to what makes Orvieto Orvieto. It will never be a question of being unaware and that is just what I hope to pass on to those for whom Orvieto is already home, and to those for whom Orvieto may eventually become home. I suppose it is also a matter of what home is to you, a place that, as Kia says in her marvelous letter, *"is a feeling, an emotion, an unspoken beauty that only you can experience yourself."*

Orvieto is more than the facade of the Cathedral glowing in the afternoon sun. Or the high tide of tourists peaking around noon and waning by four. Orvieto is not only its centuries of history, its buildings and people of the past and present. I suppose like all of life, the city is the sum of memories of each day, of knowing things will change and trying to hang on to them before they are relegated to yesterday.

Orvieto - Photo by Claudio Bizzarri

Some discover this city on the cliff anew each year, others who have lived here all their lives take it for granted. Yet for all of them Orvieto is also the Corso, with its continuous parade of people and dogs. Even in this age of cell phones, if you go up and down long enough, you're likely to run into your insurance agent or seamstress, or your travel companion who you thought you had lost. It is those who say *buon giorno* and *buona notte* and whose names you can't remember even if you have known them, seems forever. In June it is the heavy fragrance of the linden blossoms perceptible even in the center of town, the magnolia and the wisteria behind the walls of the convent garden, the small side streets and alleys, the clouds reflected in an open window, the patterns of the shadows cast by the street lights and the sheets hanging out to dry. Orvieto is also the view across the valley, with the vineyards, still golden in November, blanketing the hills punctuated by the exclamation points of dark cypresses.

Valley - Photo by Erika Bizzarri

We asked for a definition of Orvieto. Yet ultimately Orvieto consists of our individual memories – and what it is for me will not be what it is for you.

So get up early when the sky, off to one side, is reddening. Soon the sun will be shining down relentlessly, and you will be seeking the shade. The streets are still empty, a dog barks here and there behind a wall. A light goes on. A window opens to let in the morning air. Someone looks out to see what the weather is, still in undershirt and sure no one will see him. A wind suddenly ruffles through the trees and a lone car, preceded by the beam of its headlights, moves silently down the street. There's a narrow lane cut between low stone houses on the left. Or it might be on the right. Whichever one you take, you'll eventually end up with just empty space before you. It's what Henry James described as a certain shipboard feeling. In Orvieto you can't just keep on walking in the same direction. Robert Coates too, in his book on the hill towns of Italy, felt "islanded" in Orvieto, surrounded by air instead of water. The sun climbs higher, its rays breaking through the blinds and drawing people from their beds.

Or you might want to wait till after dinner. As you amble along the edge of the cliff, on the way to the elevator, you almost float out into the bowl of darkness with its scattered strings of lights and the stars set against the sky, still blue green at the horizon. Back in town, the small streets flanked by the low medieval houses have their doors open and the fragrance of grilled sausages lingers in the air. It's warm tonight, the wind has gone to sleep. Your next-door neighbor goes back into the house, returns carrying a chair. And then another one and a small table. He's soon joined by others, each bringing a chair of their own. They sit in the halo of the street lamp, softly conversing, before someone brings out a pack of cards, glasses and a bottle of wine. This is the human factor, this is what matters, people part of their surroundings. In the afternoon, weather permitting, you might just like to go to one of the parks and playgrounds. Like a friend of mine who comes for six weeks every year, you could take your knitting, settle down on a bench, watch the children playing and strike up a conversation with a grandmother, mother or even a father. It's a good way to practice your Italian. Or pull out your sketchbook, or just a book to read. A good place is what is known as the Confaloniera, more or less behind the former barracks. Or of course the former fortress next to the funicular. Or any of the benches scattered throughout the town.

Then if you just feel like wandering and perhaps focus on some specific element, there are:

the 24 churches of Orvieto to be checked off;

or you could hunt for dragons or other creatures hiding here and there on the buildings;

or you might want to photograph the medieval windows and arches;

or the door knockers;

of course there are always the views over the valley from the outer courtyards;

or the inner hidden courtyards;

staircases, inside and outside;

chimneys;

reflections.

And of course there are always the people.

Those who are no longer here

Perhaps by giving one's imagination free rein, those people are still there, unseen. That imposing unmistakable figure in a greatcoat and a wide-brimmed hat coming out of his office on Via Garibaldi is Valeriano Venturi, "l'avvocato". The lawyer par excellence. As he walks up towards the City Hall, he is stopped every few steps by someone he knows, which is practically everyone. Always, always, there is physical contact. He reaches out to take a hand, to place his hand on a shoulder, as he enthusiastically talks about the latest book he is reading, often a Latin author, or tells them how when it came time to vote whether Italy should be a monarchy or a republic. His mother had given him a copy of the American constitution to read. He was only a boy, he tells you, when the Germans occupied Orvieto and what he remembers most is always being hungry.

In front of Sant'Andrea, Gilberto invites people in for mass. You can't see him, but you know he's there even though he's still rather uncertain as to his new non- corporeal existence.

And Don Marcello, too, looms up on the threshold of the church, his bride as he calls it, ready to scold you for not doing your duty before he goes to La Palomba for a plate of ombrichelli and a glass of wine. You can't see him, but you know he's there. As usual he's arguing with Mario Bizzarri about the archaeological stones under the church, and they laugh together as Valentino arrives, taking off the extra tie he had put on because the hospital required its doctors to dress formally – forgetting he already had a tie on. No, you can't see them, but they are there.

Up on the Corso, Reno Montanucci looks up from his cashier's post – you can't see him, but he's there. Smiling, inviting you to have that cappuccino with some whipped cream and a chocolate pastry. And don't forget to pay for it.

And there is Gualverio, with that serious smile of his, cornering his workers, asking them to figure out how to make a better three-legged table.

Further up in Piazza San Giuseppe Sergio Riccetti, the Capitano del Popolo as there were no others, his beard getting longer for the procession, is sitting on a bench, his knobby cane by his side. If you want to see what the Etruscans looked like, he's a perfect example.

You can't see them, not any of them, but you know they are there. For they are Orvieto.

Up on Via del Duomo, Emilio smiles at you as you pass. How many photos have been taken of the boar's head right outside his shop? No one ever made panini better than Emilio. Artichokes in oil, truffle cream, prosciutto, all layered in a crispy bun. A gentleman, who serves his clients with the grace of a ballet dancer.

Up by the Duomo, Livio Orazio, another great name, keeps an eye out for colleagues of the past. He finds Ippolito Scalza more simpatico than Signorelli, who prides himself on wearing the latest fashions. Or Maitani who vaunts the fact that he comes from Siena. Livio completely agrees with Ippolito that one is never appreciated in one's home town.

Of course there are others, silently thronging the streets. True, you can't see them, but you know they are all there. For they are Orvieto. And soon, all too soon, I, too, will be walking up the Corso, saying "buon giorno" to most of those I pass. They may not hear me, but they will remember me and I will be there with them.

Orvieto. City of high bastions

Streets going up with steps. Climbing up.
Stairs of escalator.
Streets ending in sky.
Tiles and chimneys.
Walls. Doors. Windows. Sky.
Walls with signs of the past.
Closed up arches and windows.
Furrows in the stone.
Walls with moss.
Signs. No parking. Elevator. Escalator. Arrows.
The past mirrored, the past enclosed.
Animals. Cats. Pigeons. Starlings. Dogs. Birds.
Aqueduct.
Orvieto is its past and its present.
Its past as seen through the present.
Names of trattorias. Signs again.
A sign indicating something else.
Colors.
Different stones.
Sun gold on Duomo.
Color of moss.
Color of houses. Grey of street.
Textures.
Of tufa. Of wall. Of old door.
Permanence.
Transcience.
The town hall. The theater. The school. The churches.
But what of these do we see?
The town hall – the stairs. Horses going up.
The theater. Music.
The school. Children.
The churches. Crusades, funerals, weddings.
Weddings are the future. Funerals the past.
Orvieto without people is the past.
With people is the future. Which turns into the past.

Ring around the cliff, the Badia, Porano, the Tamburino, the cemetery, the surroundings

If you are thinking of going outside the city gates, you might begin with the ring walk around the perimeter of the cliff, partly on roads, partly on boardwalks suspended halfway down the side of the cliff. Along the way there's a cave containing carbonized fossils of trees that grew here when the area was covered with forests, thousands of years ago, although the cave is generally closed. There's the small church of Crocifisso del Tufo with a crucifix cut into the rock, and a view of the necropolis down below with a detour leading to the site. There are several entrances to the walk, one by the Albornoz fortress, at Porta Postierla, one at the bottom of Via Pecorelli, where you pass the vestiges of Porta Vivaria, there's one across from the schools, and one by Porta Maggiore. Both Orvietani and expats frequently use the ring road for their daily exercise. Originally five gates, the twelfth-century one was replaced in the 19th century by Porta Romana, the name indicating that it leads to Rome.

Then there is the **Abbey or Badia of Saints Severo and Martirio.** A place where you might want to go to be by yourself, since it invites meditation. You could take a bus to the bottom of the cliff and then walk up the road, with the ever-changing views both of the abbey and of the city left behind, close-ups of the vineyards and the tower with weeds of various kinds etched against the sky. (photo of tower) A windy day makes you feel alive as you wander around the grounds with a classical view of Orvieto seen through the great arch, all that remains of what must once have been the refectory. History and ghosts abound. The monks, whether Benedictines or Premonstratensians, are still reciting their prayers, cardinals are still silently walking through the empty halls. And perhaps even Rotruda, who promised to found the abbey when her hand remained attached to the coffin of Saint Severo. Or Matilde of Canossa who supposedly had the twelve-sided tower built in the eleventh century. You might even chance to be there for a wedding. Although certainly not of the kind where the future bride wanted to have her maids of honor pick poppies and weave them together with ears of wheat as garlands. I had a hard time convincing her that poppies wouldn't last more than an hour or so and that it wasn't a good idea.

Or you might want to hike up to **Porano** along the medieval aqueduct that brought water to the city in the 13th century from a source higher up so that it reached the fountains in the squares under its own power. Some of the stone conduits can be seen along the ring route, or in a niche to the right as one takes the escalator to the top of the cliff. And while you're in the vicinity of Porano, there's Castel Rubello, which controlled the communication route of the Via Cassia and whose history seesawed between the papal and imperial factions. The castle, much restored and now a B&B, has a church of its own and a barnyard where wheat was threshed. One can also walk to the nearby Golini Etruscan tombs, paintings from which are now in the Archaeological Museum in Orvieto, and the Hescanas tomb, with paintings still in situ. The park of Villa Paolina, in the town itself, is headquarters of the Institute of environmental and forestry biology and where Harvard has a yearly course on refugee trauma.

Or walk up the **Tamburino** where one passes the former church of Santo Spirito degli Armeni, the portal of which now graces San Domenico. There's still a public water basin for washing clothes along the way – when I was in Italy in 1956 I stayed in a tiny village in the mountains in the north and did my washing in such a public wash tub, helping the other women wring out their sheets. Refreshing on a hot summer day, but in winter with freezing weather it must have been pretty daunting.

A side road with a large tree and a bench leads to the upper entrance to the cemetery (opened 1867). There's a former Franciscan convent right outside the walls, now used by American study–abroad students during their digs, and a Jewish chapel with a menorah over the main door. Ismaele Trevis, a textile merchant, had arrived in Orvieto from Rome with his wife and three children. When his son died in 1912 he obtained permission to build the family chapel outside the Catholic cemetery. The Trevis family members eventually moved to other cities.

(I've already touched on the Jews in Orvieto and on the Cahen family). A day can be spent wandering the paths of the cemetery lined with simple tombstones bearing only the dates and names (but what a variety!) or more elaborate monuments with sorrowing angels or veiled portraits of the deceased and some with photographs of people who couldn't have been anything but contadini or laborers. And the highrise "apartment" buildings, cubicles along the walls, contrast with the family chapels in Gothic, Byzantine, or Renaissance style. The church, badly in need of repairs, was designed by Raffaelo da Montelupo, Greek-cross plan and now is used only for storage. One of the tombs I like best is the one with the portraits of the Mazzocchi husband and wife (photo of tomb), gazing straight at you (Victorian, severe, a man who ruled in the family, with a medal pinned to his lapel, she just behind, with a smile lingering on her lips) in the small square used for services on the Day of the Dead, November 2nd. (by Filippo Severati, died 1892, invented enamel painting on lava, palazzo Mazzocchi, facade 1829-30). This is also the best time to visit cemeteries in general, with tombs swept clean and with fresh flowers and lighted candles.

Mazzocchi tomb - Photo by Erika Bizzarri

Everywhere the cypresses. Whenever you meet up with groups or congregations of cypresses, unless they are lining the road leading to a villa, they are telling you: here are your ancestors, here are the people who came before you and to whom you owe thanks. Wish I could hear them tell their stories. Outside, if you are driving to Bolsena, on your left you pass the imposing fortress-like walls of the cemetery extension (1991), which I have a hard time liking. It is an early work by Massimiliano Fuksas, who was fascinated by cloud forms. Particularly striking is his Armani 5th Avenue store in New York City, inaugurated in 2009.

Back up the **Tamburino**, the old Etruscan road, for a view. Paved at the top in worn cobblestones, there was probably once an inn here whose sign was that of a drummer boy or *tamburino*. Fields and low houses alternate on either side. The beautifully restored stone house, near the top, entirely in keeping with the medieval architecture, has unusually large windows on the ground floor, behind which one can see piles of books. You might even hear a piano playing jazz. And when you're at the very top, where the way is blocked to traffic, look back and you'll have the view that appears in Brockedon's guidebook of 1834. Why don't you pick up a reproduction of his engraving from one of the shops on Piazza Duomo? It certainly won't take up much room in your suitcase. At a lecture on just how much what we see is conditioned by what we have read, or by works of art we have seen, the speaker, who had various books on Alexander the Great to his credit, insisted that my idea of Orvieto had been conditioned by Turner's painting in the Tate. In vain did I tell him that I hadn't even been aware there was such a painting. I'm not at all sure, by the way, that Turner's view was from here, for after all while he did make plein air sketches, his paintings were then studio concoctions. If he needed a fountain with women washing for his composition, in it went.
You might also try to **hike to Bolsena**. True, it's quite an outing but you can just cross the main highway and go into the woods along a path where you can encounter the boulder that split to let the holy relic from Bolsena pass in the 13th century. This is Sasso Tagliato. There are the ruins of a bridge and a rock incised with the date 1575. One wonders, who engraved it, how come he (presumably a he) had the necessary tool, and what he looked like.

You can also take an alternative route to **Canonica and Sugano**, passing through chestnut woods, past a pond and springs of mineral water. In 1895 the engineer Aldobrando Netti and the city of Orvieto made plans for the creation of a hydroelectric power plant, just below the springs that gush out at the base of the inhabited center of Sugano. In May 1901 Netti created the first electric illumination of the Mancinelli Theater. There is also a public washbasin near the crossroad to Canonica. When I first came to Orvieto, I needed someone to help me with my tiny son and the house and found Alba, who came in from 8 to 4. When she married, her sister Aurora took over. Their parents were real peasants who barely knew how to read and write. I was invited to their home in the country, where the animals were stabled under the living quarters and when you had to go to the loo – that is where you went. I remember feeling rather discomfited when Aurora introduced me as her "padrona" for I certainly didn't think of myself as her "master" or "mistress". She eventually married and had children of her own. Her family history is a typical example of how Italian society was evolving. Her parents were illiterate. Aurora had been to the fourth grade. Her children both finished university and her daughter is now a lawyer. And married to a lawyer.

Sugano for me is also Checco who was one of my husband's best diggers in the Etruscan necropolis. A tall hard-working fellow, he had been a clandestine tomb digger before being "converted" and was also known for his skill in finding water or empty places with a divining rod. He lives on in our family history.

Bricks and tiles are what characterize **Castel Viscardo**. The "factories" are well worth a visit, whether you need a new floor with "cotto" or just want to see how the clay is still shaped into bricks and tiles and fired in a wood-burning kiln the way the Romans did. Workers put a gob of clay into a form and smooth it out before setting it in a row with its brothers to dry. Once dry, it is stacked in a great kiln and a wood fire is kept burning for 3 or 4 days. These hand-made bricks have also been used in restoring ancient monuments, such as the Coliseum.

Tiles drying in Castel Viscardo - Photo by Erika Bizzarri

Closer to Orvieto itself is **Rocca Repesena,** a sort of miniature rupe or rock. It is now also known as the City of Roses for hundreds of rose bushes have been planted along the way as you climb up the steps to the top of the cliff for a view of the countryside.
There's also the other side of Orvieto. After leaving the railroad station and crossing the river, a road to the right leads to the **English cemetery** and to the site of what is known as the massacre of Camorena where the Fascists shot seven Orvietani shortly before the end of the war. Continuing on, before getting to the dam of Corbara, on the right are the ruins of the Roman port of **Pagliano** where the flood of 2012 raised havoc. Rivers were one of the main communication routes and wheat and timber were sent to Rome from Orvieto and surroundings. When the cathedral was built, the stone (red limestone from Prodo, Castellana, Suselvole, serpentine from Montespecchi, white marble from Montepiso on the way to Siena, alabaster from Parrano and the territory of Abbadia di S. Antimo) would come by river before being hauled up to the top of the plateau by ox cart. The forests furnished chestnut, oak and pine, while marble came from the quarries of Carrara and the ruins of ancient Rome.

If you're an inveterate hiker, you should download the *Caput Etruriae* book on the Orvietonews site, with indications of hikes going all the way to Perugia. Years ago my sons and some friends decided they would walk to Perugia (it's around 80 km by car) and I made them brownies as energy food. They were in their teens at the time and stayed overnight in a sheep barn. When they finally arrived at their aunt's in Perugia, she immediately put them in the tub. So don't sleep in a sheep pen on your way.

Sometimes I am asked if Orvieto has changed. One might just as well ask, "Have I changed?" Time passes. We are no longer what we were and Orvieto is no longer what it was. From across the valley it seems to have changed little except that there are now more houses along the roads in the valley with buses and cars where transportation used to be on foot.

Orvieto is its past and its present. The past seen through the eyes of the present. Most noticeable perhaps are the demographic changes. Often from around ten in the morning to just after noon you will encounter the Nigerians, who then magically vanish. Then there are those who have found work here, many from Moldavia, who walked across the mountains in search of a place that would welcome them. San Lorenzo dei Arari on Sundays is an orthodox church with its iconostasis. A friend who teaches English in a middle school near the railroad station says half her students are the children of immigrants. While she is supposed to be teaching them English, many don't really know Italian. Although their parents frequently return to their country of origin, the children have been born here and a law is pending that would give them citizenship. The young Orvietani on the other hand often go elsewhere to seek a future, even though Orvieto remains "home".

Some of the *"stranieri"* or foreigners only eventually ended up here, trial and error. Some came and never left.

Orvieto, city of high bastions. That's what it will always be, even if it now takes only five minutes to get to the top. As visitors to Orvieto, we look for the past, but live in the present with its people, its trattorias, the signs telling you where you can and cannot go. Perhaps it is this fusion that makes Orvieto such a living city – one that I call home, and for which you too will find a place in your heart.

What Orvieto means to one student

Perhaps one of the most touching testimonials to what Orvieto means comes from an Arizona study abroad student. It sums up what Orvieto is.

Letter Kia'Hod Guedes Pereira, an Arizona University study abroad student, left for "Claudio's mom" when she went back to the States.

> *What does Orvieto mean to you?*
> *This is a question that has been in the back of my head for 3 months.*
> *Orvieto is...*
> *Opportunity*
> *Adaptability*
> *Growth*
> *You are faced with yourself, one of the most frightening faces to see. You are taking the training wheels off and wobbling back and forth to stability; Some fall, some go too fast and some struggle but they always learn to ride.*
> *With our eyes wide open we see too much to understand; it is the type of beauty that makes you cry.*
> *How could a small town have such an immense impact on who we are?*
> *With my eyes wide open I have opened a treasure chest to see the life of a stranger. I have met a new person; their past, their present and their possibilities for the future.*
> *I have met myself.*
> *Orvieto*
> *The cobblestone streets I walk every day, the three-story homes that hover over me, the proud personable lives I hear and see. The rim wall around Orvieto holds all of us together like mosaics.*
> *With my eyes wide open,*
> *I have fallen standing.*
> *I have bared myself,*
> *seen myself in unfamiliar eyes and I have felt my body in a new skin.*
> *In Orvieto ...*
> *I have found and accepted myself.*

It was this town's soft touch telling me it is going to be okay and its stern grip pulling me to keep going.
As my journey comes to an end the bitter
taste of leaving lies on my tongue.
My temporary relationship has turned into a love I can't let go.
Orvieto is not easy to put into words,
it is a charming feeling that takes over.
Orvieto is a feeling, an emotion, an unspoken beauty that only you can experience yourself.
Life changing.
With eyes wide open, I came not expecting, not knowing and I found purpose.
Orvieto was an unexpected chapter in my life. All of my life, lessons, experiences, winding roads have led me here and I know I am where I am supposed to be.
A piece of me will forever be in Orvieto. I may leave but I will be back So what is Orvieto to me?
Orvieto is love, hate, cries, realizations, struggles, improvisions, adaptations, tests, excitement, challenges, fears, all experiences I would never change for the world.
Thank you Italy and thank you Orvieto.

Suggested reading

Alexander, Robert E, Elliott, John A, Pauli Bizzarri, Erika, *An Artist's Spiritual Odyssey*, University of South Carolina Press, 2018

Bassetti, Sandro. *Orvieto città aperta*, Lampi di Stampa, 2009

Bizzarri, Mario, *Magica Etruria Orvieto and Perugia*, translated by Erika Pauli Bizzarri, 2014

Calvino, Italo, *Invisible Cities*. Translated by William Weaver, Harcourt, Inc, 1974

Coates, Robert M., *Beyond the Alps: A Summer in the Italian Hill Towns*, William Sloane Associates, New York, 1961

Cryan, Mary Jane, *Affreschi Exploring Etruria*. Davide Ghaleb Editore, 2001

Cryan, Mary Jane. *Travels to Tuscany and Northern Lazio*, Davide Ghaleb Editore, 2004

Dickens, Charles. *Pictures from Italy*, The Ecco Press, 1846
Forster, E.M., A Room with a View. London: Penguin Books, 1990

Gilmour, David, *The Pursuit of Italy, A History of a Land, its Regions and their Peoples*, Penguin Books, 2012

Heseltine, Richard, *Pippin's Progress*, Silver Horsepress, 2001

Lansing, Carol. *Passion and Order: Restraint of Grief in the Medieval Italian Communes.* (Conjunctions of Religion and Power in the Medieval Past.), Ithaca: Cornell University Press. 2008

Lansing, Carol. *Power and Purity. Cathar Heresy in Medieval Italy,* Oxford Univ. Press, 1998

Lawrence, D.H., *Twilight in Italy, Sea and Sardinia, Etruscan Places*, Viking Press, inc. 1972

Ledda, Gavino, *Padre padrone*; translated from the Italian by George Salmanazar, Aperture, 1980

Mark Twain, *The Innocents Abroad*, The New American Library, 1966

Norton, Charles Eliot, *Notes of Travel and Study in Italy*
Orvieto La Città Medioevale, Istituto Storico Artistico Orvietano, 1988

Parks, Tim. *Italian Neighbors*, 2003

Parks, Tim. *An Italian Education*, 2006

Perry, David Eugene, *Upon This Rock*, Pace Press, 2020

Satolli, Alberto. Ed. Microcosmo Ceramico, *La decorazione in maiolica di Marino Moretti nel giardino della Nuova Biblioteca Pubblica di Orvieto*, Comune di Orvieto, 2014

Waley, Daniel. *Mediaeval Orvieto: The Political History of an Italian City-State, 1157-1334.* Pp. xxv, 170. New York: Cambridge University Press, 1952.

Acknowledgments

With heartfelt thanks and love to Annie Loui and Diane Charney, without whose prodding I would never have undertaken this journey, and in particular to Katherine McIver for her patient inspiring support and editing; to all my expat and Orvieto friends who are as much Orvieto as the view of the city from my house in the country.

Many thanks to Kia 'Hod Guedes Pereira for her permission to use her letter on what Orvieto means to her.

I am also eternally grateful to David Perry and Alfredo Casuso for their advice and help in getting this online and in particular for Alfredo's marvelous layout. If it hadn't been for them . . . .